# God's Healing Strategy

*Published in association with*
*Eastern Mennonite University*

# God's Healing Strategy

## An Introduction to the Bible's Main Themes

## Ted Grimsrud

*Foreword by*
James E. Brenneman

## Pandora Press U.S.

*The original name of Cascadia Publishing House*
Telford, Pennsylvania

Copublished with
**Herald Press**
Scottdale, Pennsylvania

Pandora Press U.S. orders, information, reprint permissions
*Use contact options for Cascadia Publishing House, the new name of Pandora Press U.S.:*
contact@cascadiapublishinghouse.com
1-215-723-9125
126 Klingerman Road, Telford PA 18969
www.CascadiaPublishingHouse.com

*God's Healing Strategy*
Copublished with Herald Press, Scottdale, PA; Waterloo, ON
Library of Congress Catalog Number: 00-057138
International Standard Book Number: 0-9665021-9-1
Printed in the United States by G. B. Printing, Logan Township, NJ
Book design by Pandora Press U.S.
Cover design by Merrill R. Miller

The paper used in this publication is recycled and meets the
minimum requirements of American National Standard for Information
Sciences—Permanence of Paper for Printed Library Materials, ANSI
Z39.48-1984.

All Bible quotations are used by permission, all rights reserved, and
unless otherwise indicated are from the *New Revised Standard Version Bible*,
copyright 1989, by the Division of Christian Education of the National
Council of the Churches of Christ in the USA.

**Library of Congress Cataloguing-in-Publication Data**
Grimsrud, Ted, 1954-
God's Healing Strategy : an introduction to the Bible's main themes /
Ted Grimsrud.
   p. cm.
Includes bibliographical references.
ISBN 0-9665021-9-1 (alk. paper)
   1. Bible--Textbooks.  I. Title.

BS605.2 .G75 2000
220.6'1--dc21

                                                    00-057138


10  09  08  07  06  05  04          18  17  16  15  14 13  12  11

*To the memory of my mother,*
*Betty Wagner Grimsrud (1922-1999),*
*who more than anyone else taught me that*
*nothing matters as much as love.*

# Contents

# Foreword

DEFENDING GOD AND THE GOOD NEWS of God's reign has a long and storied past. In theological circles such a defense has often been labeled "theodicy." In its simplest version, the argument goes, "How can an all-powerful, all-good God, allow evil?" Other versions of the same essential question abound. The Psalmist repeatedly asks God, "How long?" "How long will you hide your face from me? How long must I bear pain in my soul? How long shall my enemy be exalted over me?" (Ps.13: 1-2).

In relation to such agony, even Scripture comes under scrutiny and needs defense. What does a Bible reader do with conflicting stories of God in Scripture? How do we reconcile biblical depictions of God as ruthless tyrant with those of a benevolent parent? Is the God of the New Testament the same character as the God of the Old Testament? The questions pile up.

*God's Healing Strategy* is an excellent response. It is a defense both of God and of the Holy Scriptures, Old and New Testaments. As pastor, college professor, and biblical theologian, Grimsrud argues his case clearly and cogently without the usual arcane highly specialized jargon often associated with such important questions. Each chapter is chock-full of stimulating discussion points making the book a cross between a refreshing Sunday sermon and a Bible study lesson.

There is an amazing built-in healing quality to our physical bodies that to this very moment, astounds me. Our doctors can aid in this process, but healing is a basic structural component of life, as we know it. So much so, we take healing for granted, until, that is, we get terribly ill and our healing requires us to endure a long recovery—or none. Grimsrud speaks to both sides of our experience. On the one hand, he defends the basic nature of reality as one of healing or wholeness (*shalom*). On the other hand, he accounts for why healing of our own and of the world's woes often takes so long. The former is best accounted for in the Bible's view of God as Creator of a good and healthy world. The latter comes out in the Bible's vision of God as the Redeemer, Healer, Savior of a world gone awry. God as Redeemer, which depends on the first description of God as Creator, is what Grimsrud suggests is the golden thread that ties the whole Bible, Old and New Testaments, together. From Genesis to Revelation, the Alpha and Omega of biblical revelation is the story of God's healing strategy.

Still there is that nagging question, "How long, Oh Lord?" Why does God's healing strategy take so long to be fulfilled? The great blessing of this book is that Grimsrud does not sidestep that most difficult and universally asked question. To dodge such a fundamental query would be to charge God with neglect of the worst kind. Grimsrud shows how ultimate healing must happen without coercion. Like a masterful surgeon, God's healing strategy has always been to help remove obstacles to our complete wholeness so God's (super)natural power of healing can then flow through us to the world.

What God has chosen, however, is to remove obstacles through noncoercive perservering love. Given the recalcitrant nature of humans and our slow learning curve, God's loving response to evil—God's healing strategy—requires a long, slow process. God's patience joins God's love in thwarting attempts to rush the healing process by means contrary to God's character.

To his credit, Grimsrud defends God's willingness to change, to adapt to ever new situations of human failure, so God's healing strategy can take place. What is truly unchanging about God is God's perservering and patient love. To argue in traditional terms that the God of Scripture is unchanging is to make God out to be arbitrary and distant. The perfection of God does not lie in God's impassibility. The perfection of God lies precisely in God's willingness to change when love demands it.

The Bible as a whole tells the story of such a God of love.

People of God who call themselves Christian cannot simply pull Jesus out of a magician's hat, as it were, as if no one before Christ's time had understood the healing strategy of God. Jesus understood his own healing ministry and that of the church which would bear his name as part of the same old, old story revealed in his Scripture, our "Old" Testament. The incarnation of God in Christ is simply the latest, and yes, for Christians, the climactic revelation of God's noncoercive patient love, adapting as it had so many times before. This book provides its readers with a profound recovery of a central message in the Older Testament that gives meaning to the New Testament. One cannot read *God's Healing Strategy* without renewed appreciation for all of Scripture, Old and New, cover to cover.

The Apostle Paul, on trial before King Agrippa (Acts 25), had to defend his encounter with the God of his past as revealed in the Christ of his present. In much the same way, this book stands under the weight of history declaring, for all who would listen, a defense of its wild hope. In the words of the apostle Paul, which could well be those of Grimsrud, that defense rests on the "hope in the promise made by God to our ancestors, a promise that our people hope to attain, as they earnestly worship day and night" (25:6-7).

For the apostle Paul as for us, this hope lies in understanding God's healing strategy for the world as revealed in all Scripture. King Agrippa, of course, was almost persuaded by Paul's argument: "Are you so quickly persuading me to become a Christian?" (v28). Well aware of the utter patient, perservering love of God, the apostle responds, "Whether quickly or not, I pray to God that not only you but also all who are listening to me today might become such as I am" (v. 29). And so, whether quickly or not, may the defense of God and God's Scripture put forward by this small book persuade all who read it of the hope in God's healing strategy for the world.

—*James E. Brenneman*
  *Pasadena, California*
  *Lead Pastor, Pasadena Mennonite Church, and*
  *Professor of Old Testament,*
  *Episcopal School of Theology at Claremont*

# Author's Preface

WHEN I BECAME A CHRISTIAN AT AGE SEVENTEEN, I experienced an immediate change in my relationship with the Bible. What had been a puzzle became a source of practical wisdom, an encouragement for faithful living, and a constant source of intellectual stimulation. In the nearly thirty years since, I have never ceased to be interested in the Bible. And I have always found in the Bible a challenge to the commonplaces and easy assumptions which most of us in North America, all too wealthy and comfortable, tend to find ourselves settling into.

As a young Christian, I thirsted for help in understanding the Bible. I was blessed with many friends who shared such thirst, not least the woman who became my wife and continuing partner in discerning and applying the Bible's message, Kathleen Temple. Our early passion for this task continues—and is expressed in our constant conversing about biblical themes.

I also was blessed to discover numerous written resources. Two monthly periodicals always chock-full of stimulating biblically-oriented writings, *Sojourners* and *The Other Side*, served as my mentors. They introduced me to such insightful biblical interpreters as John Howard Yoder, Jacques Ellul, William Stringfellow, Dorothy Day, and many others.

A third blessing, along with friends and reading materials, came later. Kathleen and I discovered the Mennonite Church, learned to know Mennonites in our Eugene, Oregon, home community, and took the opportunity to spend a year at the Associated Mennonite Biblical Seminary in Elkhart, Indiana.

Surely the 1980-1981 school year was the most exciting ever experienced at AMBS!

Our teachers were superb. I learned the Bible from Willard Swartley, John Howard Yoder, Millard Lind, and Gertrude Roten. Our fellow-students were even better. We made numerous lifetime friends and experienced amazing hospitality, given our marginal status as "Mennonite walk-ons." An added blessing that year was an impressive roster of guest speakers who visited campus, including Krister Stendahl, Phyllis Trible, James McClendon, Tony Campolo, Allan Boesak, and James Cone.

Our time at AMBS convinced Kathleen and me to formalize our relationship with Mennonites by joining the Mennonite Church. Almost accidentally, I soon found myself pastoring, first as a Eugene Mennonite Church interim pastor. In the years that followed, my biblical education took the form of sermon preparation. I discovered that preaching provides a unique opportunity for thinking through the message of the Bible.

In a moment of inspiration (or beginner's foolishness) I decided to begin my preaching career as a Mennonite minister with an extended series on the Book of Revelation. My kind friends in the Eugene congregation spoke words of affirmation, so I took the next step of submitting versions of my sermons as articles to the Mennonite Church weekly magazine, the *Gospel Herald*. Editor Daniel Hertzler accepted my articles—an act of generosity for which I still am deeply grateful.

The series of seven articles helped open several doors for me. These included my second pastoral assignment (interim pastor at Trinity Mennonite Church in Glendale, Arizona) and the opportunity to publish my first book, *Triumph of the Lamb: A Study Guide to the Book of Revelation* (Herald Press, 1987).

My approach to Revelation, summarized briefly in chapter 13 below, reflected my application of the approach to the Bible I had learned from my teachers. I tried to take seriously the original historical setting for Revelation but asked from the very beginning what this book has to say to us today, particularly in terms of our Christian vocation to follow Jesus' peaceable way.

When we returned to Eugene in 1987, and I began pastoring there on a permanent basis, I embarked on several long-running preaching series on sections of the Bible. Probably the most interesting series for me was a year-long treatment of key texts in the Old Testament. Again I took seriously the historical setting of the passages I preached on but also focused on the relevance of these parts of the Bible for Christian discipleship. I continued the same approach when we moved on to Salem Mennonite Church near Freeman, South Dakota.

Then I began teaching at Eastern Mennonite University in fall 1996. My very first class (meeting at 8:00 a.m .the first day of school!) was Faith and Christian Heritage, a historical introduction to Christian faith. The first third of this class dealt with the Bible. I drew on my sermons to put together class lectures.

*God's Healing Strategy* is a revision of those sermons and lectures. My goal is to introduce the message of the Bible—which I continue to believe is a message of God's love and human responsibility to live lives which reflect that love. I hope this brief book may open for readers a door to much deeper and more comprehensive engagement with the Bible.

I have included an extensive list of reading resources I have found helpful over the years. Recognizing the importance of communal interaction in discerning and applying the Bible's message, I have also included at the end of each chapter some questions for reflection and discussion

This book is small but my list of debts large. I am grateful to my teachers—in the classroom and on the written page. I am even more grateful to the three congregations which provided contexts for my preaching ministry and to Eastern Mennonite University for providing the setting for my teaching ministry.

In each of these situations I have been blessed with friends who continually confirm to me the wisdom of Kathleen's and my choice to become part of the Mennonite Church. Another such friend is Michael A. King, publisher, pastor, writer, conversation partner. I am grateful to Michael for taking on this project through Pandora Press U.S. Kathleen, eagerly, and our son Johan, not always so eagerly, also have been and continue to be wonderful conversation partners in things of the Spirit.

A word yet about my mother. As a child, I was always encouraged to think for myself. I don't remember our family spending a lot of time with the Bible, though we were certainly taught to respect it. In any case, the guidance I received from my parents was largely unspoken, modeling more than lecturing.

Only as an adult did I sit down with my mother and talk much about the Bible. In her retirement, she became a Bible study leader and enjoyed talking with her theologian son about what each of us was learning. Through these conversations, though, I realized that I had learned my basic approach to the Bible from her years ago, even without her overtly articulating it. That is, I had learned from her that nothing matters as much as love—and that love provides the context for understanding everything that is worth knowing in life.

My first book was published shortly after my father's death. It was bittersweet to dedicate it to his memory—I would have much preferred him to have seen the book itself. So, when I first began making plans with Michael King for publishing this, my second book, I felt happy that I could dedicate it to my mother and give it to her to enjoy. Sadly, this was not to be. She died suddenly and unexpectedly of heart failure a little over a year ago. So once again, I have the bittersweet privilege of dedicating a book to a recently deceased parent. I hope that in some small way, this book will help others know the love of God reflected to me through the lives of my parents.

—*Ted Grimsrud*
  *Harrisonburg, Virginia*

# God's
## Healing
## Strategy

# 1

# Introduction: A Biblical Way of Seeing

### What is the Bible?

The Bible is a remarkable collection of writings. One of the final books of the Bible, the Second Letter to Timothy, provides a concise summary of how people in the Jewish and Christian traditions look upon the Bible: "All Scripture is inspired by God and is useful for teaching, for reproof, for correction, and for training in justice, so that everyone who belongs to God may be proficient, equipped for every good work" (2 Tim. 3:16-17). The purpose of the Bible is equipping people of faith for every good work, lives of service to God and humanity.

Of course, anyone who has spent time reading the Bible is well aware that understanding this massive book is a lifelong task. We find in the Bible a huge diversity of perspectives, styles, and settings. In this way, the Bible reflects human life in general—ambiguous, diverse, complex, at times difficult to understand.

In writing *God's Healing Strategy*, I am aware of the challenge we face in seeking to understand the message of the Bible. I am making a preliminary proposal here: Taking all the various threads of biblical faith together, we may discern a single overarching concern. The Bible as a whole tells a story—what I will call the story of God's "healing strategy," God's bringing

*21*

about of salvation. That is, the Bible tells the story of God's work to restore wholeness to the human/divine relationship.

I hope in this short book to provide an overview of this story, told in concise, straightforward fashion. I am suggesting an angle of sight for interpreting the story the Bible tells. I will be giving many examples from the Bible to justify this angle of vision. However, I will certainly only be scratching the surface of the Bible's testimony, even though I believe my proposal will bear up under scrutiny. My bibliographical notes represent the wider reading I have done and provide evidence of wide agreement among at least portions of the scholarly community.

Whether you accept my proposal or not, though, I hope considering it will stimulate you to further reflection on how you believe the Bible should be understood and applied to life. Following the words in Second Timothy, we all are challenged to seek to understand how the Bible speaks to our present day expressions of faith-oriented living.

I want to be clear about my own perspective. I write as a Christian—for many years a pastor, now a professor at a Christian college. I write as a Mennonite Christian—part of a tradition dating back to the early sixteenth century which has been noted for its concern with peace. However, I hope my reflections will be of interest to *anyone* interested in the Bible.

### A biblical way of seeing

The story of God's healing strategy among human beings is a subtle history. It generally is difficult to see God's hand at work in any direct way. Even some of the apparently clear instances become cloudy over time.

We need a perspective to interpret the story—what we might call a biblical way of seeing. This perspective starts with the affirmation that there is a God, a God who creates and loves this creation—including human beings created in God's image, created (like God) to be loving and in loving relationships.

But something has gone wrong. Loving relationships have been broken. Creation has been marred. Salvation is needed. God can't simply step in and by force make things right. God's healing strategy is much more subtle. God's activity is shaped by a patient, long-lasting, persevering love, a love that desires healing for all.

We may trace that strategy throughout the Bible from its first to last books. The act of creation itself, presented in the first two chapters of Genesis, was a molding of order and beauty out of chaos. Following the return to chaos through the disobedience of Adam and Eve, we read later in Genesis of the calling of Abraham, which exemplifies God's healing strategy expressed through the establishment of a community of faith.

God's healing strategy continues with the exodus of the children of Israel from slavery in Egypt, the giving of the law to shape their life as God's people, and the gift of a land in which to live out their faith. When the ancient Israelites departed from God's will for them, they received God-sanctioned prophetic reminders of that will. Finally, following paths other than God's led to the destruction of ancient Israel's nation-state and exile of the nation's leaders. In exile, though, prophets rekindled the people's hope in God's healing strategy.

God's healing strategy culminates in the life, death, and resurrection of Jesus Christ, the bringer of definitive salvation. The Bible concludes, in the Book of Revelation, with powerful visions of the final achievement of this salvation—the coming down of the New Jerusalem and the healing of the nations.

## The "Problem" of the Old Testament for Christians

We begin consideration of God's healing strategy by looking at the Old Testament. The story of faith of which Christians are part has its beginnings in the Old Testament. The biblical perspective is expressed most clearly in Jesus, but many of the truths we see in Jesus we also find in the Old Testament.

In particular, we find in the Old Testament a portrayal of God's creative love and of the main task, the main vocation, to which God calls human beings: that of living in relationship with God and expressing God's kind of creative love in our lives.

However, Christians do not always respect the Old Testament or see it as an important resource for faith. Many Christians might be surprised to see a study on God's healing strategy beginning with the Old Testament. Don't we have all we need in the New Testament?

Christians typically cite a variety of reasons for minimizing the importance of the Old Testament, such as these: The Old Testament is full of war and violence. The God of the Old Testament is angry, judgmental, vengeful, quick to anger, slow to forgive, arbitrary, altogether fearful. The Old Testament is legalistic, focusing on the letter of the law and full of detailed, obscure, extraordinarily picky rules and regulations—with fierce consequences for those who do not follow these rules to the letter. The Old Testament is patriarchal, male-dominated, from the masculine deity on down. It has little helpful to say to women nor to men who desire gender equality.

In addition to such reasons for seeing the Old Testament as problematic, Christians give practical reasons for their disinterest in the Old Testament: this material is very difficult to understand, it is boring, it is distant from our modern world. It is difficult to apply the Old Testament to present-day life. Simply that we call it the "Old" Testament implies that it is no longer important, that it has been surpassed by the message of Jesus and the New Testament (the "Christian" Testament, in contrast to the "Hebrew" Bible).

As will be clear in later chapters, I reject such arguments for minimizing the Old Testament. Rather than respond to them in detail, I will simply offer a few points in rebuttal, then *show* in the following pages how interesting and relevant the Old Testament is for those desiring "training in justice" (2 Tim. 3:16).

I propose the following three important reasons for valuing the Old Testament:

(1) The Old Testament was *the* Bible for Jesus and the first Christians. Usually when the New Testament uses the words *Bible, Scripture, writings,* or *it is written,* it has in mind the Old Testament. For New Testament writers, the Old Testament provided the content for their understanding of God and God's will. They understood their writings to complement the Old Testament, not to take its place. Jesus said he did not come to overthrow the Old Testament (i.e., the "law," Matt. 5:17) but to fulfill it, to make it clear, to revitalize it.

The New Testament, especially the life and teaching of Jesus, does give Christians a perspective for interpreting the Old Testament, for weighing what is most important, for seeing the Old Testament as pointing forward to God's fullest expression of God's will in Jesus. However, for the New Testament people, the Old Testament remains revelation from God and essential for understanding God's healing strategy, God's work to bring salvation.

(2) The Old Testament provides a rich record of the history of God's people striving to understand God, to live in relationship with God, to do God's will. It tells of the faithfulness (and unfaithfulness) of human beings who are like us in many ways. We have much to learn from these stories.

The Old Testament, in a rich and fascinating way, records various people of faith struggling to live faithfully—as such, it gives us many rich resources in our struggle to live faithfully.

(3) The Old Testament is a positive resource for peacemakers. Certainly one of the problems of the Old Testament is how much violence there is in it. However, I have become convinced that the Old Testament also contains helpful parts relating to peace.

For one thing, we need to remember that "peace" is a positive concept. Peace is not simply the absence of violence. Peace is not simply saying "No!" to warfare. The word for peace in the Old Testament is the Hebrew word *shalom*. Old Testament writers use the word shalom to refer to many positive things—wholeness, reconciliation, justice, creativity, compassion, love, empowerment, freedom. These are things to be for, to work at, to build. The Old Testament and its notion of shalom can help Christians broaden our understanding of peace and have a positive, constructive focus—to do more than simply say "no."

Another reason the Old Testament may have a special contribution to make to our peace concerns is that our avoidance of violence, of conflict, can be a problem. We may too easily be tempted to hide from conflict, to pretend it does not exist. However, to be peacemakers we must be honest and face the lack of peace, the reality of conflict and violence in our lives. We cannot overcome violence without honestly facing it.

Certainly I am uncomfortable with much of the violence of the Old Testament. Some of its stories make me cringe. However, I also believe we are better off looking head-on at the Old Testament. If we stop avoiding these difficult stories and wrestle with them in the context of the entire Bible, we may be better suited to face the challenges of real life in our world today. Our world does include conflict and violence. We may respond more fruitfully to the needs of peacemaking around us if we draw on the positive resources of the Old Testament.

## Questions for Thought and Discussion

1. Reflect on 2 Timothy 3:16-17. How have you experienced the "usefulness" of the Bible with regard to the aspects of life mentioned in these verses?

2. How do you respond to the claim that "we may discern a single overarching concern" in the Bible as a whole? What is attractive about that claim? Unattractive?

3. Is the outline of "God's healing strategy" as sketched in this chapter new to you? What is your initial response to it?

4. What do you see as the biggest problems Christians have in appropriating the Old Testament? How do you work at resolving those problems?

5. How do you react to the statement that "the Old Testament is a positive resource for peacemakers"?

## Further Reading

(For publication details here and elsewhere, see bibliography at the end of the book.)

Many writers in recent years have discovered the literary power of the Bible and written lively, engaging books about it.

For a well-written literary approach to the Bible as a whole, see Gabriel Josipovici, *The Book of God: A Response to the Bible*. Josipovici writes of turning to the Bible, having grown up with Bible stories but never having taken them very seriously. "When I turned to it I found myself faced with two very striking things: the first was that this book, though supremely authoritative for Jews and Christians, did not, when one actually read it, appear anything like as authoritarian as the *Aeneid* or *Paradise Lost*. It seemed much quirkier, funnier, quieter than I expected. The second was that it contained narratives which seemed, even in translation, as I first read them, far fresher and more 'modern' than any of the prize-winning novels rolling off the presses" (p. x).

Other insightful literary-oriented books include Herbert Schneidau, *Sacred Discontent*; Frank McConnell, ed., *The Bible and the Narrative Tradition*; Northrup Frye, *The Great Code*; and Robert Alter, ed. *The Literary Guide to the Bible*.

Walter Brueggemann is an extraordinarily prolific and consistently insightful writer on biblical theology and ethics whose works have influenced me greatly. A couple of his shorter books speak to our general understanding of the Bible: *The Prophetic Imagination* and *The Bible Makes Sense*.

Some other books on the Bible as a whole that have shaped my views include: Gil Bailie, *Violence Unveiled: Humanity at the*

*Crossroads*; Brueggemann, *Living Toward a Vision: Biblical Reflections on Shalom*; Jacques Ellul, *The Meaning of the City*; Paul Hanson, *The People Called: The Growth of Community in the Bible*; Alan Kreider, *Journey Toward Holiness: A Way of Living for God's Nation*; José Miranda, *Marx and the Bible: A Critique of the Philosophy of Oppression*; Raymund Schwager, *Must There Be Scapegoats? Violence and Redemption in the Bible*; John Topel, *The Way to Peace: Liberation Through the Bible*; James Williams, *The Bible, Violence, and the Sacred: Liberation fron the Myth of Sanctified Violence*; John Yoder, *He Came Preaching Peace*; and Perry Yoder, *Shalom: The Bible's Word for Salvation, Justice, and Peace*.

On the Old Testament and Christian faith, these books (though not all explicitly Christian) are helpful: Bruce Birch, *Let Justice Roll Down: The Old Testament, Ethics and Christian Life*; Birch, *What Does the Lord Require? The Old Testament Call to Social Witness*; Brueggemann, *Interpretation and Obedience: From Faithful Reading to Faithful Living;* Brueggemann, *Social Reading of the Old Testament: Prophetic Approaches to Israel's Communal Life*; Brueggemann, *Old Testament Theology: Essays on Structure, Theme and Text*; Brevard Childs, *Old Testament Theology in a Canonical Context*; William Holladay, *Long Ago God Spoke: How Christians May Hear the Old Testament Today*; Waldemar Janzen, *Old Testament Ethics: A Paradigmatic Approach*; Millard Lind, *Monotheism, Power, and Justice: Collected Old Testament Essays*; Lind, *Yahweh is a Warrior: The Theology of Warfare in the Old Testament*; Regina Schwartz, *The Curse of Cain: The Violent Legacy of Monotheism*; and Christopher Wright, *An Eye for an Eye: The Place of Old Testament Ethics Today*.

# 2

# The Story Begins: God Creates, Then Responds to Human Brokenness

### Genesis 1:1–2:25—
### God the Creator, Beginning the Relationship

The first book in our Bible has an appropriate name. Our word *genesis* comes from a Greek word which means "to be born." Genesis is defined as "the origin or coming into being of something." Basically, this is what the book of Genesis is about.

The book of Genesis tells us about beginnings. In the first twelve chapters we learn of many beginnings. These include—

(1) creation, the universe, the heavens, and the earth;

(2) human beings;

(3) human beings' relationship with God;

(4) the vocation of human beings;

(5) sin, brokenness, evil;

(6) God's work to bring about healing of the brokenness through calling together a community faith started by Abraham and Sarah.

Genesis 1 is especially rich in beginnings, in introductions. This chapter introduces us to numerous aspects of God, creation, and human beings.

About God, Genesis 1 tells us that God is before everything else, is independent of creation (transcendent), creative, powerful, good, life-giving, and the giver of freedom.

About creation, Genesis 1 tells us that it is good; that it comes from God; that it has meaning to God; that it is alive, growing, vital; that it is harmonious and orderly—not chaotic; and that it is distinct from God.

About human beings, Genesis 1 tells us that we are created in God's image (which means we too are creative, powerful, made to be in relationships). We are created good, not evil or sinful; humankind includes male *and* female; human beings are given responsibility, dominion, called to be stewards and care for creation; we are called to be fruitful and multiply; we are finite, dependent on God.

When Genesis one tells us that "the earth was a formless void" (1:2), we may have an allusion to pre-creation chaos. This portrayal of creation stands in contrast with other Ancient Near Eastern notions of creation in which there are battles, conflicts, a sense of inherent conflict at the very core of what is. In Genesis there is nothing of that sort—simply God fashioning creation out of the chaos, making peace out of disorder.

The point here is not creation out of nothing so much as that God is the order-giver, the *peace-maker*. The act of creation itself is the work of God-the-savior, the *shalom* (peace) creator.

Some scholars see a particular contrast here with the Babylonian creation myth that is violent to the core. That myth pictures conflicts among the gods with the one with the most brute force winning. Part of the lesson was that human beings are an afterthought and must live in constant fear of the gods (and, not coincidentally, in subordination to the king, who represents the gods).

In Genesis, creation is a peaceable act, highlighting God's love and the significance of *all* people. In this understanding of creation, there is no need for a human king.

The grand finale of the work of creation is the creation of human beings—in God's image. We may see several significant aspects of this affirmation.

The notion of "image" conveys a sense of a close connection between human beings and God. Human beings are created with unique capabilities and responsibilities. One way we might understand the "image of God," based on the context here in Genesis 1, is to see that being created in God's image means we share with God capabilities, power, the ability to create and shape the environment around us.

The main responsibility human beings are given here is to exercise "dominion" over the earth. The connotation of dominion points in the direction of stewardship, cultivation, tending like a garden.

Another significant aspect of the creation of human beings is that we read that God created human beings male *and* female. Humanness at its heart has to do with people in relationship with other people. Both genders take part equally in God's image and share responsibility for the work God has set before us. Both genders are creative, meant to exercise power in relation to the rest of creation, and to be in relationship with one another.

The picture of God and human beings in Genesis 1 includes a sense of mutuality, of relationality. God desires a relationship with these free, creative beings God has made. Human beings themselves exist as humans only in community.

The first creation story concludes with a strong affirmation—"everything . . . was very good." Creation is *good*, including human beings. God's intention is goodness, wholeness, peaceableness, justice.

The affirmation of creation's goodness underscores that the world is not inherently evil. Evil and violence are *ex*trinsic to reality. Therefore they may be resisted and we may hope and trust that God will ultimately destroy them. The heart of God and of God's creation has to do with peace, goodness, and wholeness.

The human problem does not have to do with how we are made. Our problem has to do with our perceptions, attitudes, and beliefs. Violence, pride, sloth, and more are not part of created human nature but corruptions of God's good work.

On the seventh day, God rested (Gen. 2:2). The Sabbath rhythm—work and rest—is at the heartbeat of creation itself. In this context, the Sabbath connotes a sense of completion and contentment on the part of God and also points human beings toward an attitude of trust and worship.

The overall picture is that creation is good, harmonious, and that everything fits together. This picture establishes the baseline, the starting point in relation to which what comes later (fall, sin, brokenness) should be seen.

Genesis tells us not that God was a failure in making something good which was soon corrupted, but rather that God from the start has been committed to the goodness of creation. God has been committed enough to do the work of bringing creation into being (Gen. 1). And God is committed enough to creation to remain faithful and loving and seek to restore wholeness when brokenness comes.

### Genesis 3:1–4:16—Sin and the Human Condition

Genesis 3:1-24 contains the story of the fundamental break in the relationship between human beings and God. It tells of the emergence of sin as part of the human condition, of the rise of brokenness among human beings.

The first two chapters of Genesis portrays creation as good, harmonious, the pieces fitted together by a loving creator. However, already in 2:17 we see that human beings have limits. They are created in God's image but are not God. The limit placed on them here is the command not to eat the fruit of the tree of the knowledge of good and evil.

We do not know exactly why this prohibition was given. The key point, though, is that the prohibition emphasizes that human beings are finite and subservient to God. They have limits. To be whole, they need to defer to God, to trust in God, to live within the framework God has provided. Human beings are finite. They are created to serve God.

This prohibition provides a wedge for doubts and questions to enter in. The serpent asking her questions exacerbates Eve's uncertainties and doubts. The questioner, craftiest of the wild animals, asks some troubling questions. However, his questions reflect several distortions of the situation.

The serpent distorts the situation in these ways: (1) The prohibition is rephrased as an *option*—though God had given it as a command. The serpent says, You can eat from the tree if you want to. (2) God is not talked to or with but simply talked about. God is not part of this conversation. God is removed from the picture and becomes an object "out there." (3) God speaks of death in 2:17 simply as describing a boundary. This is the cause-and-effect consequence. The serpent presents this as a threat from God. (4) The serpent misquotes God (God has not said do not eat from any tree). The woman corrects the serpent, but the possibility is now opened that she could, if she wanted, go a different way than God's.

The seeds of doubt quickly come to fruition. Adam and Eve reject their limits. They try to deny their finitude and seek to be like God (Gen. 3:6). In doing so they shatter the ordering of creation. They bring brokenness into the relationship with God.

This yielding to temptation brings about many consequences. Adam and Eve are now afraid of God. They feel shame at their nakedness. There is established a hierarchy between the man and the woman, he ruling over her. She will now experience pain in childbirth. A new struggle with bringing fruit from the earth ensues—battling with weeds and thistles. In the next chapters of Genesis we read of more consequences. Cain murders his brother Abel. Widespread sinfulness leads to the Flood. Human arrogance contributes to construction of the Tower of Babel.

There is the barren condition of Sarah, who is unable to have children.

Since then, we have seen two major consequences for human history. On the one hand, one consequence has been the continued expression of sin and evil—wars and rumors of wars, other conflicts, the deterioration of the environment, and so on. Yet on the other hand another consequence has been God's ongoing work to bring about salvation and reverse the damage done by Adam and Eve's act.

Adam and Eve are said in 3:10 now to be afraid of God, one of the more poignant effects of their fall. What does this fearfulness indicate? Their failure to trust in God, their awareness that their relationship with God has been greatly damaged, their instinct to protect themselves, and their movement from "we" to "I."

As a result of this fearfulness, we see anxiety, distance between the people and God and the people and each other, hurtfulness toward other people. Blaming others. Losing creativity. Dominating creation rather than caring stewardship. Exercising coercive power over other people.

Certainly God is judgmental here. Even more, though, God expresses mercy. Adam and Eve are not killed. They are allowed to live. They are given time and space. We can look ahead to Jesus' teaching about mercy in the parable of the Prodigal Son, and Paul's teaching about God's love even of God's enemies in Romans 5. Genesis 1–11 teaches that there is always room for a future with God.

Adam and Eve's sin resulted from their unwillingness to accept their finitude. They refused to live consistently as creatures and to recognize that only God is God. This refusal led to their *breaking* of their trusting relationship with God. When God comes to walk with them, they *hide*. The result for them, and for all who have followed them, has been struggle, alienation, and brokenness.

The story from Genesis 4:1-16 is a troubling account of two brothers. God's rejection of Cain's sacrifice seems arbitrary. However, it parallels the prohibition of eating from the tree in Genesis 2:17. The key in both places is the struggle we humans have accepting our limits and our need to accept that only God is God and that consequently our responsibility is to defer to God.

The big issue early in Genesis 4 is how Cain will respond to bumping up against these seemingly arbitrary limitations. In particular, Cain is alienated from Abel, whose sacrifice God has accepted. Cain complains to God, and God tells Cain that Cain will indeed be accepted by God "if you do well" (Gen. 4:7). God appears to be challenging Cain to be reconciled with his brother.

Cain instead gives in to his fears and frustrations. He *murders* his brother. We see here the consequence of Adam and Eve's break with God. The lost harmony leads to heightened anxiety and fear. Cain bumps up against his limits and responds not with trust but with violence. The spiral of violence is set loose.

However, as with Adam and Eve, God remains committed to the relationship. God judges Cain but also shows a measure of mercy. God allows Cain to live, gives him a new home. God gives Cain time and space. Cain still has possibilities for a future.

Genesis 1:1–11:30 begin with the goodness of creation but continues on to tell a sad story of brokenness and alienation, of human beings turning from God. It seems as if there are three possibilities for God in the face of this brokenness.

(1) *Massive punishment.* Human beings get their just reward. They rejected God so God can simply reject them. The Flood story can perhaps be interpreted as God doing just that, then realizing that this was not what he wanted after all—that his commitment to his relationship with humankind was too important. So he vows never to inflict massive punishment again.

(2) *Coerced conformity.* God could simply force people to do his will. However, that too would defeat his purposes in creating human beings to have *free* relationships with him.

(3) *Healing without coercion.* This is what God chooses. It is a long, long process by which human beings *voluntarily* return to their relationship with God. Humans will be lovingly persuaded to turn to God, not in response to force but to God's never-ending compassion and mercy.

This choice of God to pursue healing without coercion is basically the story of the rest of the Bible—culminating in the work of Jesus Christ. We do find a few cases where coercive actions (or at least intentions) are attributed to God in the Bible (e.g., the "hardening" of Pharaoh's heart in Exodus 1–15, various warnings of the prophets). However, the overall thrust of the Bible's portrayal of God's healing works shows us patient, persevering love as the core of what God does. We see God's persevering love even in the Bible's worst judgment story—the story of Noah and the great flood.

## God Continues the Relationship:
## Noah, the Flood, and the Rainbow

Genesis 9:8-17, the story of the giving of the rainbow, concludes a story which begins in Genesis 6:1—and tells of Noah and the great flood.

In Genesis 6:5 we are told that the spiral of violence unleashed in the Garden, later expressed by Cain and others, has continued, ever deepening. "Every inclination of the hearts of humankind was only evil continually."

This is followed by a remarkable statement: "The Lord was sorry that he had made humankind on the earth, and it grieved him to his heart."

A couple of key points are implied in this statement. That "the Lord was sorry for what he had done" implies a lack of total control on God's part. God is changeable. Also, God's response is one of grief. God did not first of all respond with raw anger or disgust or hatred. God grieves, feeling the kind of pain, which comes out of love and vulnerability.

The events that follow come out of God's grief. God is hurt. Something of God is broken when creation is broken. God is not so much an impersonal judge here, whose righteous honor is offended. God, much more, is an abandoned lover, a friend betrayed. God grieves. God hurts. God feels sorrow.

Out of this deep grief comes the Flood. Creation is broken, a source of inconsolable pain—so creation is *un*created. The inconsolable lover cannot stand to see the betrayer still around. The destroying waters rise and rise, the Flood goes on and on.

God concludes human sin has reached a point that warrants judgment: the Flood that almost wipes everything out. However, God decides to *continue* the relationship with human beings despite their sin.

In a nutshell, we see here that God remains committed to creation, especially to the special relationship God has with humans. This relationship has been powerfully expressed in Genesis 1: "In the image of God he created them, male and female." The story of the Flood concludes with the affirmation that God will never give up on this relationship.

The story of the Flood fascinates. God's patience with human sin ends. However, after the Flood, God vows to Noah, "I will never again curse the ground because of humankind." Yet— and this is one of crucial points to this story—human beings have not changed. God says *after* the Flood is over, "the inclination of the human heart is evil from youth" (Gen. 8:21). Human beings caused the problem by our inclination toward evil, and even after the Flood (God's rescue of Noah and his family, God's promise never to do this again) this human inclination toward evil remains.

In other words, God does not make God's promise because human hearts have changed. It appears that what has changed is *God's* heart. God gave in to anger for awhile and brought massive punishment. Genesis 7:23 tells us that God blots out "every living thing that was on the face of the earth."

The turning point in the story comes in Genesis 8:1. "But God remembered Noah, and all the wild animals and all the domestic animals that were with him in the ark. And God made the wind blow over the earth, and the waters subsided." God rescues Noah and promises not to punish in this way again—even though there is no indication that the inclination of the human heart has changed. We see evidence that the human heart has not changed in the story in Genesis 11 of the Tower of Babel.

It is as if God changes God's own mind, giving in to anger but then deciding the only way to heal creation is through persevering love. God remembers creation, decides that creation is worth redeeming, and makes a commitment to the long haul of love.

The key phrase here is that "God remembered." Throughout the Bible, God's remembering of God's people has connotations of salvation, renewed life, hope.

The waters subside. Chaos recedes. God re-creates. Life is restored. God blesses Noah and re-affirms humankind as still in God's image. God restores humankind's dominion over the rest of creation. The story ends with God's promise: "Never again shall there be a flood to destroy the earth" (Gen. 9:11).

We may draw three lessons from this story.

(1) *God changes.* The movement from judgment to mercy is not the result of humankind changing. We saw in Genesis 6:5, before the Flood, that God sees people as "evil in the imaginations of their hearts." After the Flood, in Genesis 8:21, we are told again by God that "the inclination of the human heart is evil from youth."

God's movement from vengeance to mercy happens because of a choice *God* makes. God chooses: either indulge in anger and retribution, or resolve to do something new.

We could almost say that what happens is that God sees chaos, the Flood, threatening totally to take over. Utter chaos is where retribution leads. Retribution is not the *solution* to the problems humans have created. Chaos is not overcome with greater chaos.

To turn back the chaos, God must find another way to deal with God's grief. God chooses to be with humankind, to exercise persevering love, to extend mercy that never ends. When we discuss Genesis 12 below and the calling of Abram and Sarah, we will reflect more on this.

(2) *God gives the rainbow.* The key image in the Flood story is the image of the rainbow. "God said, 'This is the sign of the covenant that I make between me and you and every living creature that is with you, for all future generations: I have set my bow in the clouds, and it shall be a sign of the covenant between me and the earth. . . . And the waters shall never again become a flood to destroy all flesh" (Gen. 9:12-13,15b).

The "bow," in the ancient Near East, is a weapon of *war*, the bow for the arrow. However, here it is a weapon of war unstrung, a weapon of war which will not be used for war anymore. God is no longer in pursuit of an enemy. God will never again be provoked to use this weapon of war to destroy the world. God's response to the brokenness of creation is now based on loving persuasion, not on brute force—seeking patiently to heal.

(3) *This story remained a living memory for Israel.* Much later, the people of Israel experienced another Flood-like experience. The great empires—Assyria and Babylon—conquered their two kingdoms of first Israel (the northern kingdom), then Judah (the southern kingdom), respectively. Many of the Israelite people were sent into exile.

The prophets interpreted this fate as judgment. The people were living in sin, with injustice, practicing idolatry and false worship. However, God met even the unjust Hebrews in their suffering and brokenness with healing love. In exile, the prophets saw the story of the ancient Flood as a picture of God's change of heart from retribution to mercy. God's mercy would meet them, too, in their time of flood and overwhelming chaos.

Isaiah 54 spells this out. "'This is like the days of Noah to me: Just as I swore that the waters of Noah would never again go over the earth, so I have sworn that I will not be angry with you. For the mountains may depart . . . but my steadfast love shall not . . . and my covenant of peace shall not be removed,' says the Lord, who has compassion on you" (Isa. 54:9-10).

God promises that what the people of faith were experiencing was not the Flood to end all floods. God's steadfast love will not leave his people. Even during their flood-like times, God's love remains. God's response to human sin and evil remains one of patience and unquenchable love.

The story of Noah and the Flood, especially its conclusion in Genesis 9:8-17 and the promise of the rainbow, tells us that God cares so much about the ongoing relationship with human beings that God will keep loving us and keep loving us—and will work in loving ways to bring us back into harmony with God. This is the kind of harmony human beings were created for.

A key word in Genesis 9:8-17, which comes up over and over is *covenant,* which means an agreement, a pledge, a compact. Basically the point here is that God is making a formal commitment not to act with such anger again. God is essentially promising to persevere with creation, to hang in there, to seek to heal this brokenness caused by human sin.

The story of our faith heritage is the outworking of this covenant established by God thousands of years ago—God's strategy to bring healing to God's broken creation.

## Questions for Thought and Discussion

1. What understanding of the nature of life can we draw from the story of creation in Genesis 1? What difference does it make to confess that creation is *good?*

2. How would you characterize the human vocation of exercising "dominion" over the earth? Is this still our vocation? If so, how might we best carry it out?

3. How do you respond to the statement that "violence . . . [is] not part of created human nature"? What implications would follow from agreeing? From disagreeing?

4. What do you understand to be the core problem in the eruption of alienation between humans and God as portrayed in Genesis 3? What is violated for this to happen?

5. Is the "fearfulness" which characterizes Adam and Eve's response to God immediately after their eating the forbidden fruit warranted? Is the change in the relationship which follows due strictly to human misperceptions of God or at least in part to a change in God's attitude toward humans?

6. How do you respond to the interpretation of Genesis 6–9 that asserts that God is *changeable*? In what sense, if at all, are we to assume that God changes? Why might we tend to resist this idea?

7. Do you find the story of Noah and the Flood to be encouraging to your faith or, instead, is it the kind of biblical story you would prefer to ignore?

## Further Reading

Walter Brueggemann's commentary, *Genesis*, provides theo logical and ethical insight and is the basis for much of my discussion. Brueggemann's reading of the Noah story especially has shaped my understanding.

Another commentary with a strong emphasis on theological application is Terrance Fretheim, *Genesis*, in the *New Interpreters Bible*. This entire series of commentaries, with supplementary essays on theology and interpretation, is consistently insightful for present-day faith and practice.

Bernhard Anderson, *From Creation to New Creation: Old Testament Perspectives*, is quite helpful on the significance of the creation accounts. So also is Jon Levenson, *Creation and the Persistence of Evil: The Jewish Drama of Divine Omnipotence*. Phyllis Trible, *God and the Rhetoric of Sexuality*, gives an insightful feminist analysis of Genesis 1–3. Robert Alter, *The Art of Biblical Narrative*, provides a literary analysis of the Book of Genesis that is full of perceptive analysis. Alter also has written a commentary: *Genesis: Translation and Commentary*. On some of the theological themes arising from the Noah and Flood story, see Terence Freitheim, *The Suffering of God*.

A unique kind of book, Bill Moyers, ed., *Genesis: A Living Conversation*, contains transcribed televised conversations among a large variety of scholars (including, among many others, Alter, Brueggemann, and Trible) ranging from evangelical Christians to committed secularists, all focusing on the book of Genesis.

# 3

# The Old Testament's Salvation Story: Promise and Deliverance

### Genesis 12:1-9—The Calling of a People

The biblical story of salvation basically begins with Genesis
12. In response to the brokenness of creation, God seeks patiently to heal. Genesis 12:1-3, the calling of Abraham and Sarah
to be a great people, tells of the beginning of God's strategy for
healing. God's strategy for healing is summarized in the words to
Abraham in verse three: "In you all the families of the earth shall
be blessed." Through what happens with you and your descendants, salvation will spread to all corners of the earth.

God's strategy for healing is to call a people, to establish a
community of people who will know God. God's strategy for
bringing about peace is another act of creation, the creation of a
community. It is through people of faith living together, face to
face, people of faith learning to love and give and take. Through
concrete *daily peaceable community life* among specific, particular
groups of people God will make peace for all the families of the
earth.

How might this be? How might this work? We see one later
promise in Isaiah 2:2-4: "In days to come the mountain of the
Lord's house shall be established as the highest of the mountains,

and shall be raised above the hills; all the nations shall stream to it. Many peoples shall come and say, 'Come, let us go up to the mountain of the Lord, to the house of the God of Jacob; that he may teach us his ways and that we may walk in his paths.' For out of Zion shall go forth instruction, and the word of the Lord from Jerusalem. He shall judge between the nations, and shall arbitrate for many peoples; they shall beat their swords into plowshares, and their spears into pruning hooks; nation shall not lift up sword against nation, neither shall they learn war any more." Here Isaiah envisions people from all nations coming to the house of Jacob (that is, Israel) to learn the ways of peace—because they have seen such peace expressed in the lives of the people of Israel.

As we have seen, Genesis 1–11 essentially gives the account of the disintegration of the human community: the breakdown of the peace, the wholeness of creation down through the Garden of Eden, Cain's murder of Abel, the Flood, and the tower of Babel—where human ambition runs afoul of God, leading to disintegration and confusion. It is as if the human race has in short order run its course, then rendered itself powerless to do anything but self-destruct. The end of chapter 11 symbolizes this movement: "The name of Abraham's wife was Sarah. . . . Now Sarah was barren; she had no child" (Gen. 11:29, 30).

As we read these verses now, we can see that they point both backward and forward. They are a watershed. On the one hand, we read here of Abraham and Sarah's lack of a future. Sarah is barren. They will have no children—no one to carry on their line. They will disappear at death. Their deep despair symbolizes the fate of grasping, self-oriented, cold-hearted humanity living apart from God as portrayed in Genesis 1–11.

We who know where the story goes in later chapters, though, see this first mention of Abraham and Sarah in Genesis 11 as pointing forward. We know that despite appearances to the contrary, Abraham and Sarah do have a future.

In 12:1 we hear God's speech, God's word to Abraham. This is a word of hope: "I will make of you a great nation." You will have countless offspring. God's Word once again creates life out of chaos. God promises Abraham and Sarah a future. And through that promise, God also guarantees all peoples a future. "In you, Abraham, all the families of the earth shall be blessed." God's healing strategy for the human race will be funneled through Abraham.

God calls into being a people, a community of faith. God's purpose for calling this people has to do with blessing "all the families of the earth" (Gen. 12:3). This is God's strategy for healing—the creation of a community, the calling of a people to know God's love and to share that love with the rest of the world.

We can see here three important points, which help us understand the story of faith. These points continue to be relevant throughout the story we are considering in this book. First, God brings newness for his people. Second, God uses God's people to help others find this newness. Third, God is committed to continuing this strategy over the long haul.

(1) *God brings newness for his people.* The community of faith God calls together is based on these people knowing God's love and mercy. God promises newness to Abraham and Sarah. They are promised a transformation. Sarah is barren. She cannot have a child. There will be no descendants. There is not hope for the future. They are "no people."

Into this barrenness, God speaks newness. The present reality of being "no people" will change. Abraham and Sarah will be a people. God says, "I will make of you a great nation, and I will bless you, and make your name great, so that you will be a blessing" (Gen. 12:2). And God does bless Abraham and Sarah. God gives them a child. They become the grandparents of many; the great-grandparents of many—all people in the Jewish and Christian traditions. And these people know God's mercy and show evidence of that mercy to the wider world.

The Old Testament does tell us about unfaithfulness. So does the New Testament. So does church history. However, the Old Testament, the New Testament, and church history also tell of at least some faithfulness, of people who know God, of many expressions of peace, wholeness, healing, shalom. And the promise of total healing remains.

God said to Abraham, "I will bless you." The first move is God's. God brings newness. The first reality is God's mercy, God's gift of life, God's promise of a future.

(2) The second part of God's strategy for healing is that after bringing fresh life to his people, *God uses his people to help others also experience this newness.* God says to Abraham, "I will bless you," then "I will make you a blessing for others." God's strategy for healing, bringing peace and wholeness to God's beloved creation has been to use the community of faith to share with others the wholeness they are finding, the newness God has brought them.

The story of ancient Israel gives mixed messages on this score. At times Israel fought with neighbors, even on occasion oppressed neighbors. Too often Israel's people did not truly experience God's newness in their midst, so there was no light to show to the nations, no blessing to share.

This remained the case for the followers of Jesus. The Christian church inherited the vocation of Abraham and his descendants—to be a blessing to all the families of the earth. However, Christians also have fought with and even oppressed their neighbors. The church at times has not experienced God's newness in her midst and has had no blessing to share.

Yet amid many failures, the promise to Abraham has remained in effect: God will use Abraham's descendants to bring healing and salvation to people of all nations. God continues to use people and communities of faith as part of this work of making peace far and wide, part of this work of blessing all the families of the earth.

(3) The third point from the story of God calling Abraham is that *God is committed to staying with this strategy over the long haul.* People tend to find it difficult to be patient. We see so much brokenness around us. We wonder, what is the use?

God's promise to Abraham, God's healing strategy of calling a people to know and to share newness happened more than 3,000 years ago. God is still patient. God still perseveres. God's long-suffering love knows no end. God is in this for the long haul. The fact that we still look to the story of Abraham to inspire us—this one insignificant nomad is the ancestor in faith to millions millennia later—shows that God has sustained the healing strategy for a long time. We may wonder whether it is really going anywhere, but that faith still lives on indicates that God remains committed to the work of salvation.

God's calling of a people back in the time of Abraham included two elements. "I will bless you," God said, "so that you will be a blessing." These remain the two elements of God's calling of people— "I will bless you . . . so that you may be a blessing." God's strategy for healing to bring newness to people of faith, then to ask them to share that newness—and patiently trust that God will, in time, fulfill God's promise to heal creation.

### Exodus 1–15—God Brings Deliverance

We have in Exodus 15 the account of the crossing of the Red Sea, the celebration of the exodus from slavery in Egypt to the hope of new life ahead in the Promised Land. Throughout the Bible, and ever since, this moment has been recalled and held up as a basis for hope. God does liberate from bondage. God does give new life. This is a crucially important memory.

The last part of the book of Genesis tells how Abraham's great-grandson Joseph ended up in Egypt, sold into slavery. In time, though, Joseph is freed and rises to leadership in Egypt as the right-hand man of the king (Pharaoh). Joseph's father, Jacob, his eleven brothers, and their families eventually follow Joseph. At first they are in Pharaoh's favor. However, after a while Egypt comes under the rule of a new king, "who did not know Joseph" (Exod. 1:8). This Pharaoh returns the Israelites to slavery.

Exodus 2:23-25 tells of their situation. "The Israelites groaned under their slavery, and cried out. Out of the slavery their cry for help rose up to God. God heard their groaning, and God remembered God's covenant with Abraham, Isaac, and Jacob. God looked upon the Israelites, and God took notice of them." God remembered the promise, the covenant with Abraham. God remembered that this people were meant to be a blessing for all the families of the earth.

The next several chapters tell how God liberates the children of Israel from slavery. We read of Israel's great leader, Moses. His part of the story begins with his exile from Egypt, his childhood home. Moses then returns and becomes a leader of the Hebrew people, who are slaves in Egypt under the iron hand of Pharaoh, the Egyptian god-king.

Moses asks Pharaoh to let the Hebrews go; Pharaoh refuses. Moses then coordinates his interaction with the Pharaoh with God's performance of several wonders designed to impress Pharaoh and to get him to change his mind. God sends water being turned to blood, then frogs, gnats, flies, disease, boils, thunder and hail, and locusts—and finally dense darkness. Pharaoh at first refuses to reconsider then says the people can go but not the livestock. Moses says this is not good enough. This enrages Pharaoh, who says he will not reconsider any more.

So, the final plague occurs. Every firstborn child and every firstborn animal in Egypt is put to death—except those of the Hebrews, because the death angel "passed over" them. Pharaoh finally relents and lets the Hebrews go. Then he changes his mind and chases them. As the Egyptian army readies to pounce on the Hebrews, whose backs are to the Red Sea, the sea opens up and the Hebrews pass through. When the Egyptians follow, the Sea crashes down on them. Finally Pharaoh faces defeat and the Hebrew people are set free. Exodus 15 celebrates that final victory: "The Lord has triumphed gloriously" (Exod. 15:1).

The Exodus was a crucial part of God's healing strategy. It is an important memory for biblical faith. Old Testament writers often evoke, or report the evoking of, the memory of God's deliverance. God loved you, God delivered you, God brought you salvation—praise God. Let God's love for you move you to love others. Remember how God treated you while you were being oppressed—so you do not oppress others.

Three elements of the exodus story are particularly important to the Bible's overall story: first, God is a God who *liberates* the oppressed. Second, God's acts of salvation are *not* achieved through military action. Third, the Hebrews *reject* the unjust ways of empire.

(1) First we learn *that God is not primarily a God of the rich and powerful,* a God who supports authoritarian kings; rather, God is one who liberates slaves, who reaches out to the needy.

The God of the exodus is not a God of kings. This is not a God of the Pharaohs, of people in power, of people who lord it over others. This God, unlike other gods, is not a projection from the king, a way merely to reinforce the king's power. Rather, the God of the exodus is a God of *slaves.* This is a God who gives life to the lifeless, hope to the hopeless. This is a God who hears the cries of those being treated like nonpersons, those being treated only as tools to increase the king's wealth.

(2) We also learn from the exodus that *God's will for salvation is not expressed through human military action.* The hero here, God's human servant, is Moses. Moses is not a general, a leader of armies and commander of weapons of war. Rather, he is a weapon*less* prophet whose authority is based solely on him speaking for God. He began his career utterly inept, murdering an Egyptian and being forced into exile. He stutters and needs his brother, Aaron, to speak publicly for him.

The Israelites experience salvation by the direct involvement of God, not by their having more powerful horses and chariots. Egypt's arrogance and violence are seen in how Egypt trusts in weapons of war. That is a false trust. Israel finds salvation by trusting in God alone.

The Hebrews did not defeat Pharaoh by their own strength. God used miracles in nature (the plagues, the parting of the Red Sea) to bring about liberation. The center of power in this new society lay not with the generals and the warriors, but with the people's God. That the power rests with God means that the things God values most—mercy, compassion, caring for the powerless and outcast, just distribution of resources—are what matter most in the society, not the increase in wealth and power for the already wealthy and powerful. There is not a warrior-king whose military victory only brings him more wealth and power. The people with the most status are the weaponless prophets, those who best discern the will of the liberating God.

(3) We also learn from the exodus that Israel is called not simply to leave Egypt behind, *but to reject Egypt's unjust ways.* Egypt represents *empire* as a way of life, trusting in weapons of war, and oppressing and enslaving people. Egypt accumulates wealth and treats many people like things to be used and then destroyed. When the Law is given to the Israelites, much of the Law is explained and defended in opposition to Egyptian cruelty. One of the harshest criticisms the prophets make of Israel later on is that Israel had become like Egypt—unjust, materialistic, oppressive.

Egypt is not simply left behind—Egypt is rejected. Right from the start for the Hebrew people, we see competing ideologies. Egypt and Pharaoh stand for the human will-to-power. Israel and Moses stand for God's loving justice. Egypt and Pharaoh stand for life lived in fear, self-protectiveness, trusting in brute strength, exploiting others however one can. Israel and Moses stand for life lived in trust in God's mercy, openness to others, caring more for relationships than material possessions, treating the powerless with respect.

We see in the Old Testament "salvation story" two distinct themes. First is the call of Abraham and Sarah, God's promise to them that God will bring salvation. We see here a gift of newness in the context of barrenness. We see the establishment of God's plan to use the community of faith to help bring this kind of newness to all the families of the earth. This calling of Abraham and Sarah is the first step in a long, long process of God's persevering love that is doing a *long* work of bringing salvation.

Second, we see in the exodus the intervention of God to bring salvation to God's people. God gives liberation from slavery in Egypt and eventually gives the people the land of Canaan to live in. The exodus establishes God as a God who liberates the oppressed. God's salvation does not come through human power politics and humans coercing other humans. God's salvation leads to a rejection of the values of empires such as ancient Egypt.

## Exodus 20:1-17—
## God's Directives for Faithful Living

As the children of Israel traveled through the wilderness on their way to the Promised Land, God spoke to them through Moses, giving them the law—God's directives for faithful living.

The law was given to provide political structure for the delivered slaves so that the effects of that deliverance could be sustained. The law provides an "ordering" for the people of God, a framework for on-going faithful living according to God's shalom. In addition, God gave the Promised Land so these people could settle down and establish an on-going society that would live out the fruit of the exodus liberation. The on-going faithful living required a *place.*

The goal of all this was for these people to be a light to the other nations and thereby be a channel for God's shalom to spread to these nations. In other words, the context for the law included two crucial affirmations.

(1) Salvation is by *grace*, God's mercy, God's act of deliverance. The law comes *after*—not as a means of earning salvation but as an additional work of God's grace, a resource for ordering peaceable living in the community of God's people.

(2) The intent, ultimately, is to lead to universal shalom, to bless all the families of the earth (God's healing strategy). Exodus 19:6—"The whole earth is mine . . . You shall be for me a priestly kingdom." "Priestly" implies *mediator*. Israel mediates God's presence to the "whole earth."

Exodus 20 gives us the initial statement of the law: the Ten Commandments. I want to reflect on the sixth commandment as representing the whole: "Thou shall not kill." This command has been used to legislate pacifism. God *commands* us not to kill. We must obey or we will be punished. Others argue that this command only specifically means "you shall not murder" and hence has no direct relevance for issues of warfare or capital punishment. Still others would say not only is this not a rule outlawing all violence, it actually implicitly sanctions certain kinds of violence. It actually provides a rationale for capital punishment and "just" wars. Those who break this law not to murder deserve death, and it is up to those representing God to see that they get it.

The first point, that the sixth commandment legislates pacifism, seems legalistic and externally oriented. The opposite view, that the sixth commandment actually implicitly sanctions "legal" violence runs up against the bumper-sticker slogan—why do we kill people to show that killing is wrong? This view seems to tie God to the rule of an eye-for-an-eye. God then seems more or less forced to respond to violence with a new act of violence. Yet the God of the Bible is specifically spoken of as being free in general and free of this particular law in particular (e.g., God's response to Cain, Noah, and Lot).

A better way to approach this commandment is to ask first, what does this commandment tell us about God? Exodus 20:2 tells us that God prefaces the giving of the law with this self-affirmation: "I am the Lord your God who brought you out of the land of Egypt, out of the house of slavery." This prologue emphasizes in the strongest terms that God is a God of mercy; this mercy, which calls together the people out of love, lies behind all that follows.

Hence, the point of the commandments is not establishing absolute, impersonal, even coercive rules which must never be violated. The point rather is that a loving God desires on-going relationships of care and respect with these people God delivered out of suffering and oppression.

The sixth commandment, "thou shalt not kill," then essentially tells us that life is God's. This loving, delivering God is the giver of life and the ultimate determiner of the outcome of life. It is not for human beings to usurp God's dominion over life. It is not for human beings to name the time and season for life or death.

The general implications of this affirmation evolve along with one's understanding of the character of God. When God is seen as more vindictive, more retributive, then this commandment can be consistent with appropriately enforced capital punishment and holy war and other types of judgment. This would parallel the judgment of Sodom and Gomorrah. In that ancient story, God listens to Abraham but still punishes those evil cities.

However, by the time of the prophets—especially Hosea and then the second half of Isaiah—God is seen in different terms. Rather than continuing the cycle of violence, God finds other ways of responding to evil; more through suffering, ever-enduring love than retaliation. The expression of God's persevering love reaches its culmination in Jesus Christ, the lamb of God, the prince of peace. God responds to violence without adding to the violence: God finds a way to break the cycle and establish true justice—not based on an eye-for-an-eye until every eye is plucked out but based on genuine healing and reconciliation.

So "do not kill" has an increasingly broad application, culminating in a notion of a God who acts lovingly (not vindictively) toward enemies. "Do not kill" is not an external rule to follow by force of will. It is a call to discover God's mercy for oneself and let that mercy so shape our awareness that we see that all life does belong to God, who desires the best for every being.

Paul's interpretation of the law in Romans 13 makes clear the deepest meaning of the law not as rule-following, but as being open to God's love and finding ways to express that love toward others: "The commandments . . . are summed up in this word, 'Love your neighbor as yourself'" (Rom. 13:9).

## Questions for Thought and Discussion

1. Do you believe that the biblical notion of *election* (chosenness) is an asset or a liability to present-day faith-based peacebuilding work?

2. In light of historical clashes between Christianity and Judaism, what might Isaiah's vision of "many peoples" coming to Zion to learn the ways of peace (Isa. 2:2-4) look like today?

3. Do you think God's work for peace among humans depends upon the faithfulness of the community of God's people? Why or why not?

4. What evidence (if any) do you see for God's long-haul involvement in the healing of creation?

5. How do you understand the plagues from Exodus that led to the liberation of the Hebrews from slavery in Egypt? What seems most important about those events? Most troubling? How do you reconcile the liberation of the Hebrews with the suffering of the Egyptians?

6. How important for you in your interpretation of the exodus is the idea that the liberating God of the Hebrews is proposing an anti-empire ideology?

7. If following the law is understood most of all as a *response* to God's mercy (not as a means to gain God's favor), what implications might this have?

8. What role do you understand the Ten Commandments to have in your life? The overall Old Testament law?

## Further Reading

On Genesis, see the further reading note from chapter 2 above. In addition, Walter Brueggemann, *The Land*, provides a theologically and ethically sophisticated analysis of the issue of God's promise of land to God's chosen people. On Israel's calling to be a light to the nations, see Thomas Cahill, *The Gifts of the Jews: How a Tribe of Desert Nomads Changed the Way Everyone Thinks and Feels*.

On Exodus, Brueggemann's commentary, *Exodus*, in the *New Interpreters Bible*, as one would expect, provides profound theological and ethical insight. Terence Fretheim, *Exodus*, is also a strong theological commentary.

On the social and political aspects of the exodus story, see Millard Lind, *Yahweh is a Warrior* and *Monotheism, Power, and Justice* (especially the essay, "The Concept of Political Power in Ancient Israel"); George Pixley, *On Exodus: A Liberation Perspective*; José Miranda, *Marx and the Bible*; Michael Walzer, *Exodus and Revolution*; and J. P. M. Walsh, *The Mighty From Their Thrones: Power in the Biblical Tradition*.

Walter Harrelson, *The Ten Commandments and Human Rights*, is an ethically and theologically sensitive interpretation and application of the Ten Commandments. More general discussions of the law in the Old Testament include, Dale Patrick, *Old Testament Law*, and Millard Lind, *Monotheism, Power, Justice*, section II, especially the essay, "Law in the Old Testament."

# 4

# Kingship and
# the Need for Prophets

MUCH OF THE EXPERIENCE OF ANCIENT ISRAEL with the institution of human kingship was not happy. Israel's institution of human kingship stood in tension with Israel carrying out her calling to be a blessing for all the earth's families.

Israel's experience of kingship may be summarized in four points: (1) the people's inability to live with God as their only king; (2) their choice to install a human king; (3) the failure of Israel's greatest king, David, to remain faithful to God; (4) King Solomon's transformation of his role into authoritarian kingship, vindicating the warnings Israel's great judge, Samuel, gave early on about the dangers of human kings.

After the children of Israel were freed from Egypt, they wandered forty years in the wilderness. They struggled even then with whether they truly wanted to follow God's ways or not. Finally, led by Joshua, they were ready to take the next step and settle in the land God provided for them. God's special calling for these people remained the same as it had been from the beginning when he called Abraham and Sarah: to be a blessing for all the families of the earth—by showing them a better way of living, an alternative to might makes right, a different way than survival of the fittest.

After Israel settled in the Promised Land, their political system was a de-centralized association of different "tribes" or clan-

groups. When Israel on occasion—such as attacks from surrounding nations—needed a stronger, larger organization, leaders called "judges" would arise and unite the tribes for awhile.
Gideon and Deborah were two of the best judges. Gideon exem-
plified how this system worked. He led Israel to victory. Then
the people wanted to make him king. But he refused: "I will not
rule over you, and my son will not rule over you; the Lord will
rule over you" (Judg. 8:23). *God* is the only king you need.

However, the system did not always work well. The book of
Judges tells mostly of judges who were unimpressive. The book
tells of times of increasing chaos in Israel. It concludes, "In those
days there was no king in Israel; all the people did what was right
in their own eyes" (21:25). *This is the first step; Israel's inability to
live with God as their only king.*

## 1 Samuel 8:1-22—Turning Toward a Human King

First Samuel continues this story. Samuel himself actually is
a good judge, an effective judge, faithful to the ways of God and
powerful for God's justice in Israel. Things get better, but only
for a while. The beginning of the passage from chapter eight
points toward a return to chaos: "When Samuel became old, he
made his sons judges. . . . His sons did not follow in his ways, but
turned aside after gain; they took bribes and perverted justice" (1
Sam. 8:1-3). Then, the leaders express their concern that they
need a warrior-king to lead Israel in the face of a perceived threat
from their enemies, the Philistines (1 Sam. 8:20).

So, it is not surprising that in the face of a fear of returning
again to chaos, the Israelites (or at least their elders) propose
something different. They approach Samuel demanding that he
"appoint for us a king to govern us, like the *other nations*" (1
Sam. 8:5, emphasis added). They respond to fear of chaos with
desire to impose *order*, centralized power, control. *This is the second step: the people's choice to install a human king like the other
nations.*

For Samuel, accepting kingship seems too much like what the Israelites knew once before—the kingship of Pharaoh in Egypt. Pharaoh kept them as slaves. For Samuel, going the way of kingship would be a return to slavery.

When Israel's elders come to Samuel asking for a king, he responds with strong words. He tells them it is a bad idea, a short cut. Instead of working harder to live with God as their only king, they try to take the easy way out and give a human leader ultimate authority.

Samuel insists that Israel's elders will regret their choice. "These will be the ways of the king who will reign over you: he will *take* your sons and appoint them to his chariots and to be his horsemen, and to run before his chariots . . . He will *take* your daughters to be perfumers and cooks and bakers. He will *take* the best of your fields and vineyards and olive orchards and give them to *his* courtiers. He will *take* one-tenth of your grain and of your vineyards and give it to his officers and courtiers. He will *take* . . . the best of your cattle and donkeys, and put them to his work. You shall be his *slaves*. In that day you will cry out because of your king, whom you have chosen for yourselves; but *the Lord will not answer you* in that day" (1 Sam. 8:11-18, emphasis added).

Samuel knows about kings from the stories of the children of Israel in Egypt. He knows the kings of the surrounding nations: Canaanite kings, Philistine kings, the kings of the nations. He knows that they take and take and take. He finds it shocking that the elders would want a king, "so that we may be like other nations" (1 Sam. 8:20).

Samuel senses that the elders don't realize what they will be getting into. He tells the elders that, under their king, they will in effect return to Egypt. "You shall be his slaves."

Samuel adds, though, that this time something *will* be different. Back then, in the great events told of in the book of Exodus, the people's movement toward salvation from slavery began when they cried out in their grief and despair. "Out of the slavery their cry for help rose up to God. God heard their groaning, and God remembered his covenant with Abraham, Isaac, and Jacob. God looked upon the Israelites, and God took notice of Israel" (Exod. 2:23-25).

Back then, God heard their groaning—and God took notice of them. That was then. The people of Samuel's time are in the Promised Land because God heard their groaning. If they turn to human kingship now, though, they will groan again. They will return to slavery. However, something will be different. "The Lord will not answer you in that day." God will not respond to their groaning.

Basically, Samuel warns that having a king will result in a radical change in Israel's society: (1) the redistribution of wealth and power, concentrating it in only a few hands with poverty for the many as a result (in contrast to the ideal of each family having its own land); (2) the militarization of the society with the establishment of a permanent standing army and a warrior class (in contrast to a society which trusted in God for its security); and (3) a general conformity with the social patterns of the surrounding nations (instead of being the alternative society God had created from the freed slaves to be a light to the nations, not simply another nation).

Samuel's voice, however, is not the only one in Israel. He doesn't convince the elders. We are told in 1 Samuel 8 that God ultimately, though certainly grudgingly, yields and gives Israel a king. Why does God do this? We are not told. We may conclude that it had to do with God's respect for the freedom of God's people and with the likelihood that the people would learn lessons from this experience. Also, we learn from Deuteronomy 17:14-20 that there is some hope that Israel will have a different kind of kingship.

The picture of the model Israelite king in Deuteronomy 17 includes the following:

(1) Limitations are placed on the power of the king, with the intent to avoid tyranny and the danger of the king's assuming God's place as ruler of the people. These limitations include restricting the king's wealth, not allowing him to marry foreign wives, and limits on building up a military system.

(2) The point is to require a full and undivided allegiance to the Lord. Limits on wealth and horses are meant to prevent pride and ambition. Prohibitions on marrying foreign wives are intended to prevent worshiping the gods of other nations.

(3) The king is to be a model Israelite. He is to be on the same level as everyone else, following the same laws, showing the way to faithful living.

We see clearly in the actual events that follow Israel's turning toward human kingship that Israel's first three kings (Saul, David, and especially Solomon) do not measure up to the standards in Deuteronomy 17. And these are the best of Israel's kings.

Some immediate good comes from Israel's change, including increased order. However, ultimately, human kingship contributes to Israel's unfaithfulness to God's will that they order their life around God's mercy.

The Bible as a whole tells us that God's people are called to live with *God* as their only king. Human kings, human nation-states, deserve only limited loyalty. It took ancient Israel awhile to realize this, however. Even the greatest of Israel's kings, King David, was worthy only of limited loyalty and was corrupted by the kind of power people tend to give human kings.

Samuel's words in 1 Samuel 8 basically go unheeded. The people want to be like the other nations. They want someone who will "go out before us and fight our battles" (1 Sam 8:20). God agrees with Samuel that this is a bad idea and tells Samuel to warn the people of what they will be getting into if they insist on a king. Yet God does allow them to have a king.

## 2 Samuel 11:1–12:15—
## The Rise and Fall of King David

Israel's first human king is Saul. Samuel seeks Saul out, and God blesses Saul. However, Saul fails. Saul departs from God's wishes. His power slips away, and he becomes more or less crazy. He clings to control, commits major blunders, experiences great pain, and causes great pain for others.

In the meantime, a young man named David enters the scene. Saul soon recognizes David as his great rival and realizes that God's favor has left Saul and now rests on David. Saul resists this and does his best to eliminate David.

David avoids Saul's attempts to do him in. David bides his time. He does not need to grasp after power. He realizes that God is with him, that God has called him and will give him the kingship all in good time. Eventually, Saul's craziness does him in. He kills himself. David is anointed king and solidifies his position with some major victories over the Philistines.

An important example of David's faithful attitude is his relationship with Abigail, the beautiful and intelligent wife of a rich man named Nabal. Nabal is an unsavory character who insults David. Abigail intercedes with David and wisely prevents him from taking revenge and doing evil. Shortly thereafter, Nabal dies. Then, the text says, in a morally legitimate way David "sent for and wooed Abigail, to make her his wife" (1 Sam. 25:39). Here David did not need to take and grasp. He could wait and trust in God's timing.

Things go well for David. Perhaps Samuel's fears about corrupt kingship are unwarranted. David leads the armies to victory. He establishes a family. He gains favor with the people. He trusts in God and gives God credit for his success. Israel progresses on the way to prosperity, moving toward peace and well-being.

Then, however, comes the turning point. Samuel's fears are realized. Conflicts with Israel's enemies continue. Second

Samuel 11 tells us: "In the spring, at the time when kings go out to battle, David sent Joab with his officers and all Israel with him; they ravaged the Ammonites and besieged Rabbah. But David remained in Jerusalem" (2 Sam. 11:1-3). *But David remained in Jerusalem.* We are not told why. We are only told that he sends his top general, Joab, out to lead the fight.

We had been told earlier that Israel sought a king who would "go out before us and fight our battles." Here we learn it is the time of the year "when kings go out to battle." But David remains in Jerusalem. He is now relying on others to do his work.

What follows happens quickly. David remains at home while his soldiers go to fight his battles. He is outside, resting in the sun, when he spots a beautiful woman, Bathsheba. No matter that she's married to one of his key officers. No matter that he is also married. He must have her, and he *takes* her. David takes. Samuel's warning is fulfilled. The consequences are deep and long lasting. *This is the third step in Israel's experience of kingship: the failure of Israel's greatest king to remain faithful to God.*

Samuel had warned that the king would take and take. David enjoys this moment of basking in his overwhelming power and in his sense that he truly is in control of his own fate. David takes. He takes another man's wife. Up until now, David hasn't been a taker. God has given to him. David's wife Abigail, the people, they also have all been all happy to give to him. Now he takes.

Bathsheba informs David she is pregnant. Her husband, Uriah, has been away, fighting David's war. David is the only possible father. So David hurriedly summons Uriah back home, hoping he will lie with his wife and provide David with a cover. Uriah, though, remains with his fellow soldiers out of loyalty to them and their hardships. He doesn't visit Bathsheba. David's only way out is to see to it that Uriah is killed in battle. Then David can legally marry Bathsheba. David gives the orders. Uriah dies.

David tells his top general, Joab, the person directly responsible for Uriah's death, "Do not let this thing be evil in your eyes, for the sword devours now one and now another" (2 Sam. 11:25). Don't let it be evil in your eyes . . . But someone else sees things differently: "This thing that David had done was evil in the eyes of God" (2 Sam. 11:27).

God sends Nathan the prophet to tell David a parable. Nathan tells of the poor man who had nothing but a little lamb that he dearly loves. It was like a daughter to him. But a rich man takes the poor man's lamb away. The rich man did not want "to take one of his own flock" to feed to a guest. "David's anger was greatly kindled against the [rich] man. He said to Nathan, 'As the Lord lives, the man who has done this deserves to die; he shall restore the lamb fourfold, because he did this thing, and because he had no pity'" (2 Sam. 12:5-6).

Nathan minces no words in his response to David: It is "you, King David, you are the man! Thus says the Lord, the God of Israel: I made you king, I gave you everything, house, wives, leadership of Israel. If that had been too little, I would have added as much more. Why have you despised the word of the Lord, to do what is evil in his sight?"

Nathan tells David that he broke three main commandments—thou shalt not covet, thou shalt not commit adultery, and thou shalt not kill. David *coveted* another man's wife. David *committed adultery* with her. Then David *killed* her husband. God passes judgment on David. "Now, therefore, the sword shall never depart from your house, for you have despised me." (2 Sam. 12:7-12)

David, to his great credit, responds to God. He repents. "I have sinned against the Lord," he cries.

God's judgment relaxes somewhat. David stays alive. He remains king and his son Solomon succeeds him to the throne. Things are never the same, however. David is never the same, and Israel is never the same. From now on, Israel will be plagued by violence and injustice. The violence begins immediately. David's own sons fight against each other and rebel against him.

David's fall is a tragic moment. He was so gifted. He was given so much. Ancient Israel's best chance of serving as a light to the nations goes up in flames. The next few centuries are a sad litany of one corrupt king following another (with precious few exceptions). Rather than serving as just one unfortunate case, David's act of taking becomes the norm. Samuel was right— even the best king ends up taking and taking.

David's story is all too familiar. Power-over others so often leads to corruption.

David inspires fascination. He was a genuine human being. He had powerful strengths, and he had deep flaws. To some degree, he is truly a hero. The final picture, though, is that David's way was a detour. Even if David himself had not fallen, a later king would have. The institution of kingship, that is, kingship like that of surrounding nations, kingship focused around the power of the sword, results in brokenness, cynicism, and despair. The kind of world God wants, the kind of creativity, wholeness, liveliness characteristic of the kingdom of God simply cannot be established on the basis of a brute kind of power.

We see this in a later passage, which refers to David. Isaiah 9 refers to the house of David, but to a successor to David who actually goes a different way altogether. The first David was the greatest of Israel's warriors. But under the leadership of this new David, according to Isaiah 9, "all the boots of the tramping warriors and all the garments rolled in blood shall be burned as fuel for the fire" (Isa. 9:5). The new David will lead God's people in the ways of peace, not in the ways of brute power.

This new David, Christians confess, is Jesus. Jesus is a prince, not of warfare as the first David, but the Prince of *Peace*. Rather than *taking* being at the root of his kingly activity, Jesus focuses on *giving*. He gives mercy, respect, dignity. This is true of the woman caught in adultery. Jesus respects her, forgives her, and sends her away free to live a meaningful life. This treatment stands in contrast with David's luring a woman into adultery, murdering her husband, and catching her up in a life which proved to be anything but free—treating her with anything but respect.

The first David was a man with bloody hands. Certainly, as kings go, David showed integrity, vulnerability, a willingness to repent and to accept the consequences of his actions. His actions, nonetheless, resulted in continued violence, strife within his family, and a legacy of scheming, using people, and ambition.

Jesus has been called a "king" (Messiah), a successor to David. However, he was very different from David. Jesus received power only because he refused to grasp for it. He had several opportunities to claim some kind of political power. Satan tempted him with the kingdoms of the earth (Luke 4:5-8). The people wanted to seize him and make him king following some of his mighty works (John 6:15). But Jesus said no. He could not serve God and at the same time grasp for power. Jesus refused to shed blood. Jesus refused to grasp after political power.

Jesus offers an alternative kind of power. A power based not on being *over* people, but a power based on a quest for God's truth which sets us free. Jesus shows a power based on a profound trust in God's goodness and God's care.

## 1 Kings 1:1–11:13—
## King Solomon and Power Politics

One fruit of David's style of kingship was the emergence of his son Solomon as the next king of Israel. The story of Solomon presented in the Bible is in many ways flattering to him. He is portrayed as a man of great wisdom. However, if we look closely at the story, especially from the perspective of the core message of the Bible about God's healing strategy, we see that Solomon does not emerge with an unblemished reputation. By reading the story closely, we see Solomon as a sophisticated, power-seeking, ruthless leader, who as much as anyone moved ancient Israel toward its tragic ending.

What did Solomon do? (1) He ruthlessly eliminated his opponents. (2) He built a standing army. (3) He began forced labor. (4) He gathered wealth for himself. (5) He entered alliances with other nations and worshiped their Gods.

Solomon was not David's legal heir. He had an older half-brother, Adonijah. But through shrewd scheming, Solomon becomes king. Those who are loyal to the older traditions side with Solomon's brother—indicating that Adonijah had legitimacy on his side. However, once Solomon gains control, he wastes no time in establishing his power and eliminating any potential opponents. He executes Adonijah and Adonijah's main ally, old Joab, who had been David's top general. And Solomon sends Abiathar, a powerful priest, into exile.

Once in power, Solomon expands his authority. He reorganizes social structures toward much greater centralized control. He institutes rigorous taxation to expand his treasury. He begins to draft soldiers, to expand the collection of horses and chariots into a large, permanent army with career military leaders. And he also decrees a policy of forced labor for his twenty-year building project of constructing the temple and his palace.

These practices go against what had been written about kings earlier. The Book of Deuteronomy, in chapter 17, reports that Israel's kings were explicitly commanded not to accumulate wealth for themselves. Samuel warned that the kings would build standing armies, take the best of the produce of the people, and make them slaves. This is precisely what Solomon does.

Deuteronomy 17 explicitly stated that kings must not gather horses, gold, or silver for themselves. Solomon did all these things. He was renowned for his wealth.

Solomon also cultivated ties with other countries. He had hundreds of wives—women from many nations, one of the great harems of all time. Perhaps Solomon was simply a terrific lover.

However, more likely, his marriages were for political purposes. Through his wives he gained international status.

Again, this is precisely what Deuteronomy tells the king not to do. "He must not acquire many wives for himself, or else his heart will turn away" (17:17). We read in 1 Kings 11 that indeed Solomon's heart did turn away. His many wives influenced him to worship other gods. "His wives turned away his heart after other gods; and his heart was not true to the Lord his God" (1 Kings 11:4).

God warns Solomon in 1 Kings 9:6-8, "If you turn aside from following me . . . and do not keep my commandments . . . but go and serve other gods and worship them, then I will cut Israel off from the land . . . and the [temple] I will cast out of my sight. . . . This [temple] will become a heap of ruins."

This is indeed what happens. Solomon does turn aside from following God. "His wives turned away his heart after other gods; and his heart was not true to the Lord his God" (1 Kings 11:4). In time Israel is cut off from the land and the temple becomes a heap of ruins.

Solomon, like David, has many good characteristics. He is not nearly as sensitive to God as David, however. In the end, he shows no sign of turning back to God's ways. His priorities are worldly power and prestige.

Israel continued to have kings for some years. But that direction was a dead end. The kings often hindered God's healing strategy. The vision for God's work of bringing salvation to the whole earth was kept alive mostly by the prophets.

## Questions for Thought and Discussion

1. What do you find attractive—and unattractive—about Israel's decentralized political structure during the time of the judges?

2. How do you understand the Hebrew elders' desire for a human king? Why did they want this? Can you imagine alterna-

tive scenarios for how they might have ordered their common life without human kingship? In practice, what would it mean for us to live with God as our only king?

3. Do you think the model for human kingship outlined in Deuteronomy 17:14-20 is feasible in the "real" world?

4. What is your overall impression of David? What is most attractive in the story of his life? Most unattractive?

5. Do you think David "got off too easy" in terms of consequences for his affair with Bathsheba?

6. What lessons might we learn from the story of David about the dynamics of power in human social relationships? Is David's giving in to temptations and *taking* and *taking* a message that power inevitably corrupts?

7. How do you respond to the chapter's portrayal of Solomon? Do you see him more as a "hero of faith" or as one who added to the corruption of ancient Israel? What criteria matter the most in this evaluation?

## Further Reading

Gabriel Josipovici, *The Book of God*, contains an excellent discussion of the tensions portrayed in the Book of Judges, in the time before Israel had a king. On Israel's vocation as an alternative political structure to the power politics of the Ancient Middle East, see Norman Gottwald, *The Tribes of Yahweh: A Sociology of the Religion of Liberated Israel, 1250–1050 B.C.E.* and George Mendenhall, *The Tenth Generation: The Origins of the Biblical Tradition.*

On the transition from the tribal arrangement to monarchy, see Walter Brueggemann's commentary, *First and Second Samuel,* and Robert Polzin's insightful literary study, *Samuel and the Deuteronomist.*

Mendenhall's essay, "The Monarchy," is a concise, pointed analysis of the consequences of Israel's turn toward human kingship. Patrick Miller's commentary, *Deuteronomy*, gives an insightful interpretation of the kingship passages in Deuteronomy 17.

Brueggemann's *First and Second Samuel* provides an extensive and critical examination of King David, his strengths and weaknesses. Further reflections on David from Brueggemann are contained in *David's Truth in Israel's Imagination and Memory*. Brueggemann's *Prophetic Imagination* is the basis for my critique of Solomon. See also, Brueggemann, *1 Kings*.

# 5

# Prophetic Existence:
# Covenant and Conversion

*T*HE HISTORY OF ISRAEL'S KINGS is told in the books of First and
Second Kings, supplemented by various books named after
prophets, especially Isaiah, Hosea, Amos, Micah, and Jeremiah.
The two history books are called the books of Kings. In reality,
though, the central characters in these books are the *prophets*.
The kings might have been the big shots, but the people who
keep alive awareness of who God is, what God's will is, and who
express godly power are the prophets.

For the prophets, the biggest problem was people's tendency
to practice the wrong kind of religion. They did faithfully attend
to religious rituals. They went to the temple regularly. They offered sacrifices. They were, on the surface, religiously faithful
people. However, they were missing the mark, according to the
prophets. They were deaf and blind to God's true will.

God willed that their communities be places where people
lived respectfully, compassionately, honestly, and peaceably with
each other; that is, where all the people could live meaningful,
fulfilling lives. When *injustice* characterized the communities,
when some people were exploited so that others could gain more
and more wealth, when the weak and marginal people (widows,
orphans, non-Israelite strangers) were hurt and exploited—then
the nation missed the mark. The nation, despite being religiously
active, rejected God's ways.

I want to make three points about the prophets' message. (1) They took a stance of *disbelief*, of *suspicion*, of *critique*, toward the kings and the powers-that-be in their unjust society. The world is not the way the kings say it is. The prophets challenged unjust kings. (2) The prophets preached the importance of justice to God—and God's hostility toward injustice. (3) They taught that, no matter what, God continues to love God's people and to desire their healing.

## 1 Kings 21—
## Prophetic Existence: The Battle with Baal

*The first point is that the prophets challenged unjust kings.* God willed that the community be a place of genuine justice and wholeness for *all* the people. God's will remains in effect even when the great king demands something else.

We see this in the story of Naboth, Ahab, and Elijah from 1 Kings 21. What we do not learn from the stories in the Bible is that King Ahab was one of the greatest kings in the entire history of ancient Israel—at least in terms of power, wealth, and fame in the rest of the ancient Near East.

King Ahab wants Naboth's vineyard. At first he offers to buy it or exchange it for another vineyard. His offer, however, reflects his lack of respect for the inheritance practices of Israel. The land does not simply belong to Naboth. He refuses to sell it because it belongs to God and is for the use also of Naboth's parents and his children and their children. It is his inheritance. This term *inheritance* contrasts with Ahab's term, *vineyard*.

Inheritance has to do with recognition that the land is the Lord's. The land is the Lord's and is cultivated by the family through the generations for their livelihood. The Lord wills that the land stay in the family so that they will not be dispossessed and future generations made landless. When all families have their own vine and fig tree to cultivate, the community will be healthy. That health is what inheritance is about.

Vineyard, on the other hand, as used by King Ahab, views the land as a commodity, something simply to be bought and sold with little concern for the wholeness of the entire community. Those who are wealthy and powerful may accumulate more and more. The other people become landless, disinherited—a recipe for poverty and vulnerability.

Naboth refuses to part with his inheritance. He tells King Ahab no. Ahab does not like that. He has Naboth falsely accused of blasphemy and then executed. Ahab takes the land. His assumptions is that since he is the king he can do whatever he wants.

Now the God of the Bible does not simply act to impose God's will on human beings. God works for salvation by lovingly calling for people of faith to choose to follow him. In looking earlier at the story of Noah and the Flood, we suggested that the Flood story symbolizes a turning point in the heart of God. After the Flood, God decides not to impose divine will by brute force; this leads to more chaos. God decides to do the work of salvation by persevering love and mercy.

The work of the prophets highlights God's patient love. The main weapon God has against corrupt kings such as Ahab simply is the word of the prophets, reminding people of God's will and exposing the violence and injustice of this corruption for what it is. God does not use the power of the sword but the power of truth spoken to the people.

We see God's approach in the story of Naboth's vineyard. King Ahab has Naboth killed and goes down to the vineyard to take possession of it (1 Kings 21:16). The all-powerful king will have his way. But ... not so fast. Ahab meets an old acquaintance when he gets to the vineyard, the prophet Elijah. Elijah had confronted Ahab before and had been forced to flee for his life.

Ahab remembers Elijah. "Have you found me, O my enemy?" (1 Kings 21:20). Indeed I have, says Elijah. The Lord has told me the injustice you have done to Naboth. *You* are the troubler of Israel. You are the one who has disregarded the Lord's commands. You are the blasphemer—not Naboth. And you, King Ahab, will suffer the consequences. When you live by injustice, trusting in brute power, the chances are high that you will end up being overpowered yourself.

To his credit, Ahab does respond. He humbles himself. We are not told that he changes his ways. But we are told that because of his response, the disaster waits until after his death. The word of the prophet has had power.

For Elijah, as for prophets to follow, the key concern is to remind people about God. He reminds Ahab of God's will for human life, as expressed in God's commands to do justice, walk humbly with your God, be merciful.

The prophets' message certainly is negative—be suspicious of kings and people in power. King Ahab is all too typical. Do not blindly trust their claims but test them thoroughly in light of God's revealed will. But the prophets' positive message is even stronger: remember who God is, remember what God has done for you, remember what God's will for your life is.

Much of what the prophet is about is *sight*. How do we see the world? Are we genuinely seeing things in light of God and God's will for human life?

### Amos 2:6–5:24—The Prophetic Faith: God's Justice

*The second point about the prophets is that they spoke of the importance of God's justice—and God's hatred of injustice.* Here is where the prophet Amos comes in.

The basic problem in ancient Israel under the kings was that society had changed tremendously from what the great leaders Moses and Joshua and Samuel had taught the people God wanted. Their hope had been for a vine and a fig tree for every family. The society as a whole would be most healthy when each family worked its own land, when *all* people were prosperous— none too rich, none too poor.

But things changed after Samuel's time. Some people became quite rich, and many others grew very poor, dispossessed, and mistreated.

The prophet Amos expresses a harsh indictment, speaking God's Words. "They sell the righteous for silver, and the needy for a pair of sandals—they who trample the head of the poor into the dust of the earth, and push the afflicted out of the way; father and son go in to the same girl, so that my holy name is profaned" (Amos 2:6-7). Amos charges that Israel's society is unjust. The main moral trait which describes the society is "*in*justice."

What are the dynamics of injustice? One is *depersonalization.* The problem here is that people with power and wealth treat other people as *things.* They do not treat others as fellow human beings, fellow believers, people to be treated as brothers and sisters, all of whom worship the same God. Rather, the rich treat the poor as having little value. For the rich creditors, money has more value than people. The rich sell the needy into slavery because the poor cannot pay back the small amount needed to pay for a pair of sandals.

Injustice requires depersonalization. We find it much easier to hurt or disregard people we have depersonalized than people with whom we have a relationship or toward whom we feel empathy, compassion, a sense of connectedness.

A second dynamic is *exploitation.* Amos fumes: "They . . . trample the head of the poor into the dust of the earth, and push the afflicted out of the way; father and son go in to the same girl" (Amos 2:7). Exploitation has to do with using someone else to one's own advantage or to satisfy one's own desires regardless of the cost to that person. In Amos' day, that meant economic exploitation. It also meant sexual exploitation—the ages long sad story of men overpowering women.

The third, perhaps surprising, aspect of injustice, in Amos' eyes, is *religiosity.* This is the worst of all. Shockingly, Amos sees depersonalization and exploitation going hand in hand with active religiosity in Israel. The powerful people not only hurt the weak in the name of increased power and wealth; they assume that God is blessing them. They believe their power and wealth are a sign of God's blessing.

In the face of this injustice, Amos offers a corrective. His solution is *not* to turn to religious practices. God says, "Even though you offer me your burnt offerings . . . I will not accept them; and the offerings of well-being of your fatted animals I will not look upon" (Amos 5:22). The solution to the crisis is not to be found first of all at the houses of worship or through their religious practices.

"Seek me and live," God says, "but do not seek Bethel, and do not enter into Gilgal or cross over to Beer-sheba; for Gilgal shall surely go into exile and Bethel shall come to nothing" (Amos 5:4-5). Bethel, Gilgal, and Beer-sheba were three of the main religious centers in Israel. However, that is not where God is to be found in this time of crisis. Amos says seeking God in the religious centers will only make things worse.

One of the people's worst sins is to be faithful in external forms of religion and unfaithful in how they treat each other. When you are unjust, going through the motions of worshipping God only makes it worse. The solution is *not* to be found in the religious centers.

"Seek the Lord and live . . . you that turn justice to [bitter poison]" (Amos 5:6). Here's the key—begin to *live* according to God's will. Turn away from the acts of injustice which happen far too often. "Seek good and not evil, that you may live; and so the Lord, the God of hosts, will be with you, just as you have [been claiming]. Hate evil and love good, and establish justice in the gate; it may be that the Lord, the God of hosts, will be gracious to [you]" (Amos 5:14-15).

"Establish justice at the gate" is one concrete, practical way to turn toward God. The gates were small courts where exploited people could find recourse. In Amos' time, though, they had been corrupted. The poison of injustice is being expressed at this basic level. "Establish justice at the gate;" give the weaker people a chance to resist their exploitation; treat them honestly and fairly.

Amos makes the solution to Israel's crisis clear. "Let justice roll down like waters, and righteousness like an ever-flowing stream" (Amos 5:24). Amos calls for justice and righteousness. He challenges an unjust society to turn back to God. That is their only hope of finding life, of escaping the approaching calamity.

The justice imagery in Amos 5:24 helps us understand what God's justice looks like. God's justice is ultimately about healing and salvation, about life: "Let justice roll down like waters, and righteousness like an ever-flowing stream" (Amos 5:24).

Amos does not say, "Let justice roll down like thunder." The Canaanite god, Baal, was the god of thunder. Baal symbolized brute force. That was why Baal was identified with all-powerful kings. Thunder was associated with overwhelming power. But Amos opts against this image.

Amos also avoids saying, "Let justice roll down like a sword." Throughout history, the sword has been associated with justice. The ones who enforce justice do it with the sword, with the power to deal out death. Amos does not say let justice roll down like a sword.

"Let justice roll down like waters" is what Amos does say. Justice has to do with water, which is to say justice has to do with life. The people of ancient Israel were desert dwellers. They knew droughts. They knew the life-giving power of water. Their lives were precarious in the desert and depended on water, a scarce and extraordinarily valuable resource. "Let justice give us life."

When Amos asks for justice to roll down like waters, he calls for Israel's society to enhance life, especially to enhance life for those who are depersonalized and exploited. To do justice is to support life. Amos adds, by way of emphasis, let "righteousness [roll down] like an ever-flowing stream." For a desert people, an "ever-flowing stream" is an amazing resource, a stream that contains water *all* the time, a stream that doesn't dry up. God's justice, God's righteousness, is an even more amazing resource. Even in the face of faithlessness by the people, God does not quit. God's love endures; it does not dry up. God keeps working to make things right, to heal brokenness.

God's justice does not simply oppose sin. God's justice wants to bring *healing* in the face of sin. God's justice wants to make whole that which has been broken. The prophets proclaim that the goal of God's justice is healing. God's justice has to do with life. God's justice is God's response to brokenness in the world—a response that does not delight in punishment but only in offering salvation.

God's justice is primarily corrective, restorative justice. God's goal is reconciliation, the restoration of life-giving relationships between God and his people and among all the people (rich and poor alike) of the faith community. Injustice must be opposed and resisted, for the sake of God's healing strategy, which is for all people.

### Hosea 11:1-9—The Prophetic Faith: God's Love

*The third point about the prophets' message, especially seen in Hosea 11, is that no matter what, God continues to love God's people and desire their healing.*

At the beginning of the eleventh chapter, Hosea recites the basic historical realities of ancient Israel's existence. He starts with the assumption that Israel is God's *child*. The parent-child dynamic—the tender love of a mother and infant, the father teaching the child to play ball, the parents providing food and shelter, affection and discipline, education and exhortation—captures at least something of how God and Israel were connected.

"When Israel was a child, I loved him, and out of Egypt I called my child" (Hos. 11:1). We see throughout the Old Testament how central the exodus was to Israel's identity and Israel's understanding of God. God freed the poor enslaved Hebrews from Egypt. The first move was God's—and it was a move of mercy. The basic reality was God's *love* for Israel.

Israel did not have to prove herself before God would love her. Israel did not have to gain God's favor to know God. God took the first step out of pure mercy—"out of Egypt I called my child." God did not demand that Israel *earn* his love. You are my child and I love you and always will. You do not have to earn it.

God did not demand that the children of Israel earn his love. However, God did ask that they live mercifully themselves, treating each other with the care and respect God had shown them. God did ask that the children of Israel live in relationship with God.

The story tells us, though, that Israel was not able to remain committed to God's ways. "The more I called them," God says in Hosea, "the more they went from me; they kept sacrificing to the Baals [to other gods], and offering incense to idols" (Hos. 11:2).

The prophets warn of judgment to come. Others disagree—those who tell the people simply to come and worship; even while their way of life shows rejection of God's will for them. Those religious leaders will especially be judged. The basic idea is this—you keep rejecting God's will for your lives and you will suffer the consequences. Cause and effect.

Here, however, Hosea presents God saying something more than simply judgment following disobedience. "How can I give you up, Ephraim? How can I hand you over, O Israel?" Ephraim is one of the tribes of Israel. The question God is asking of his people is basically, Can I simply let you go, my child, after all that I have done for you? Can I simply write you off?

"How can I make you like Admah? How can I treat you like Zeboiim?" These were two cities, according to Genesis 19, destroyed along with Sodom and Gomorrah. Can I simply wipe you out in judgment? If we were dealing with a God whose primary characteristic was vengeance, the answer would be yes, God, you can wipe us out.

However, judgment and vengeance are not God's words here. "My heart recoils within me; my compassion grows warm and tender. I will not execute my fierce anger; I will not again destroy Ephraim; for I am God and no mortal, the Holy One in your midst, and I will not come in wrath." God says, "No, I will not simply act in anger and vengeance. I will not treat you like Sodom and Gomorrah. What will determine my actions is my compassion, my love for you—not my anger." Why does God do this? Because, "I am God and no mortal." God does this because of God's character. God does this because ultimately God is a compassionate God, God desires healing, not vengeance. God desires salvation, not punishment.

The Old Testament does at times picture God as being violent, judgmental, fearful. But here in Hosea we see something different. This is the type of God Jesus taught his followers to call Abba. This is a God who acts with mercy and compassion because it is part of God's very *nature* to do so.

Jesus' message echoes that of Hosea. God loves you. Your unfaithfulness will not destroy that love. God will not treat you like Sodom and Gomorrah, but God continues to offer you healing. God offers salvation. God does not coerce people into salvation. If you choose to live without God as the center of your life, if you choose not to let God's mercy shape the way you live, you will not know God's goodness and mercy.

There are consequences to saying no to God. However, God continues to leave the way back open. The message of the prophets, and the Old Testament as a whole, is ultimately a message about God's love. Jesus could freely quote the Old Testament when he taught about God's kingdom, about salvation, about God's love, because like Jesus the Old Testament teaches about God's love.

"God so loved the world that he sent [Jesus] so that whoever trusts in him shall not perish, but shall have eternal life" (John 3:16). John 3:16 relates closely to Hosea 11:8-9. "God so loved the world." "My compassion grows warm and tender." I will not act in anger, because I am God. My will is not vengeance, my will is that whoever trusts in my love shall live. The prophet Hosea tells us that in the face of ancient Israel's unfaithfulness, God responds with love, still seeking to bring about healing.

The Old Testament, then, does provide the basic framework for our faith. God responds to brokenness and sin and evil by intervening among human beings to bring salvation. God does this because God is motivated most of all by love and compassion.

## Questions for Thought and Discussion

1. What parallels, if any, do you see between the prophets' critique of life in ancient Israel and ways a present-day prophet might critique life in our contemporary world? Are the basic issues much different? How are religious people "missing the mark" today?

2. What social consequences follow from people losing their "inheritance" (i.e., their possession of land)? Why would it matter to God that *all* families have their own vine and fig tree?

3. Reflect on Amos' juxtaposition of religiosity and injustice. Is it conceivable to you that active religiosity could coexist with insensitivity toward, even support for, unjust and oppressive social dynamics?

4. What would be ways you would like to see our society become more "just" (that is, more life-enhancing)?

5. Do you think the prophet's warnings of judgment *describe* the inevitable processes of alienated living or *prescribe* direct action by God? Are there analogies in the modern world?

6. Hosea expresses a sharp critique of Israelite idolatry. Do you think that idolatry is a problem in our setting today? If so, how is it manifested?

7. In Hosea 11, we read of God's mercy and compassion being expressions of God's *holiness*. How does this picture fit with your understanding of God's holiness?

## Further Reading

General works on Old Testament prophecy include Abraham Heschel's powerful and passionate study, *The Prophets*; Robert R. Wilson, *Prophecy and Society in Ancient Israel*; Gerhard von Rad, *The Message of the Prophets*; and David P. Reid, *What Are They Saying about the Prophets?* Moshe Weinfeld, in *Social Justice in Ancient Israel and in the Ancient Near East*, compares the understanding of social justice in the writings of ancient Israel with other ancient Near Eastern understandings, concluding that Israel's understanding centered on concern for marginalized and vulnerable people.

On the confrontation between Elijah and Ahab, and the prophet/king dynamics in general, see Walter Brueggemann, *1 Kings* and *2 Kings*; G. H. Jones, *1 and 2 Kings*; and Jacques Ellul, *The Politics of God and the Politics of Man*.

On Amos, Shalom Paul, *Amos: A Commentary on the Book of Amos*, is comprehensive and theologically and ethically sensitive. See also Robert C. Coote, *Amos Among the Prophets*; James Luther Mays, *Amos: A Commentary*; Robert Martin-Achard, *God's People in Crisis: Amos*; Donald Gowan, "Amos" in the *New Interpreter's Bible*; and James Limburg's commentary on Amos in *Hosea—Micah*. Millard Lind's essay, "Transformation of Justice" in *Monotheism, Power, Justice*, argues that biblical justice is restorative more than retributive. See also Howard Zehr, *Changing Lenses*.

On Hosea, Renita Weems, *Battered Love: Marriage, Sex, and Violence in the Hebrew Prophets*, gives an ambivalent interpretation. See also, Walter Brueggemann, *Tradition in Crisis: Hosea*; James Limburg, *Hosea—Micah*; and H. D. Beeby, *Grace Abounding: Hosea*.

# 6

# God Remains Committed to Healing

## Hope in Exile—Isaiah 40–55

The Old Testament tells us that, as a collective, the ancient Israelites did not heed the message of prophets such as Amos and Hosea. The people (led by the kings) did not change their ways. They did not turn from injustice toward justice. The prophesied consequences came to pass.

With the book of Jeremiah, we read that the Israelite nation was wiped out as well as why it was. The center of the religious life, the temple, was destroyed. The center of their political life, the king's palace, was destroyed. Many of the people were killed and many others were shipped away to Babylon to live in exile.

The future of God's people hung in the balance. A key element of Israel's survival as a community of faith had to do with *hope*. Only with hope would the people remember God's healing strategy. Only with hope would the people realize that amid the rubble, nonetheless, God remains God. God still wants them to live out God's will, serving as a light to the nations (Isa. 42:6). Only with hope would the people realize that God does not need a state (a political institution) nor a temple (a religious institution) to bring about healing in the world.

All God needs is a people still willing to turn to God and to seek to follow God's ways. Israel, consequently, needed words of *hope* to rekindle their awareness of God, and that their calling from God was not ended. God still calls on them to be a light to the nations to the ways of mercy and justice.

Words of hope were precisely what the book of Isaiah offers beginning in chapter 40: "Comfort, O comfort my people, says your God. Speak tenderly to Jerusalem, and cry to her that she has served her term, that her penalty is paid."

Isaiah 43 contains more powerful words from God. You have been suffering, you exiles, "*but now* thus says the Lord, he who created you . . . do not fear for I have redeemed you; I have called you by name, you are mine" (43:1). But now, things have changed. Through the brokenness comes hope for wholeness and healing, through the confusion comes clarity as to God's love. The promised chaos did come, as Hosea, Amos, Jeremiah, and other prophets had warned. But after that—God's mercy endures. Hope for healing follows chaos.

The prophet brings amazing words from God. In the barrenness and despair of exile come words of astonishing hope. God has not abandoned you. God does not hate you. God lives. God still loves you.

What we have here is a surprise along the order of the surprise awaiting Peter, Mary Magdalene, and the other disciples on Easter morning. The surprise is this: God has not abandoned you. God does not hate you. God lives. God still loves you. Words of astonishing hope.

The story of ancient Israel is in many ways sad, tragic, filled with grief. Ultimately, though, it is a story of hope. As the prophet, speaking for God, proclaims, the story of ancient Israel shows that God's love remains in effect. God's love brings healing—even after sin and brokenness have run rampant. The story of ancient Israel is one of hope because it climaxes in Christ's victory over death itself. The beautiful Advent hymn, "O Come, O Come, Emmanuel" makes clear how Jesus is the culmination of the Old Testament story. Here Jesus is called Emmanuel,

Dayspring, Rod of Jesse, Key of David—all Old Testament images.

One of the ancient Israelites' biggest problems was difficulty remembering who they truly were. The Israelites struggled to understand and rest secure in their identity as God's people. They all too often lived in defiance of that identity.

The Book of Judges tells us that the people frequently did that which was right in their own eyes. The chaos which resulted led Israel to take on a human king, like the other nations. The great Judge, Samuel, warned that that would not work, but the people insisted.

Indeed Samuel was right. The people, generally led by the kings, did go the way of the nations, forgetting their calling as God's people. They built large standing armies and relied too much on horses and chariots, the weapons of war, for their security. Kings such as King Ahab led the way in overturning Israel's economic practices which had been geared toward each family having its own vine and fig tree—that is, each family having the means to gain their livelihood from their own farms and orchards. Ahab led the dispossessing of the many for the sake of concentrated wealth and power in the hands of the few. The people also tended to practice a religion that gave them comfort and a false sense of security as their society became increasingly unjust.

Israelites simply forgot who they were. In Isaiah 43, the prophet reminds the people of several things about their identity. The Lord has created you. You are creatures of the Lord, the God of Israel. You are not creatures of the Canaanite god, Baal. You are not meaningless specks of dust. You are the Lord's people. "I have called you by name, you are mine" (43:1).

To remember, to understand, to be clear about this identity is crucial. Isaiah expresses certainty that hope comes from *God*. Hope is a gift of this loving, creative, compassionate, persevering God of Israel. Hope is based on realizing that God's mercies endure forever. If you are not clear about your identity as God's people, as people created by and named by God, then you will not be clear about God's persevering love. You will be tossed around by competing ideologies. You will be motivated by fearfulness and anxiety. You will tend to base your identity on things other than God's love—things such as gathering possessions, lording it over outsiders, or nationalism and power politics.

Isaiah 51:1-3 offers a challenge. "Look to the rock from which you were hewn, and to the quarry from which you were dug. Look to Abraham your father and to Sarah who bore you; for he was but one when I called him, but I blessed him and made him many. For the Lord will comfort Zion; God will comfort all her waste places, and will make her wilderness like Eden, her desert like the garden of the Lord; joy and gladness will be found in her, thanksgiving and the voice of song."

These verses tell us several important things. "Look to the rock from which you were hewn"—look to God as your creator who made you and blessed you as good and gave you responsibilities to share God's care and love with the world.

"Look to Abraham and Sarah"—look to the way God has cared for those who have gone before and look to the tradition of God's people of which you are part.

"The Lord will comfort Zion"—look to the promises of God to bring healing, to bring joy and gladness. Clarity about our identity as God's people feeds hope, feeds a sense that the future is meaningful and will be fruitful.

Israel experiences a shattering loss of its physical world. The temple, the king's palace, the great city of Jerusalem—all lie in ruins. The people suffer in exile. In the context of that deep trauma, the loss of their world, actually, the prophet proclaims once again God's love.

The prophet proclaims words of comfort indeed. When God says to the people, "You are precious in my sight, and honored, and I love you" (43:4), God is not speaking to faithful people or to successful people or to morally upright people. God is speaking to the people who have been judged and traumatized because of their faithlessness, because of their failure, because of their immorality. It is to these low-lifes that God says, "You are precious in my sight, and honored, and *I love you*."

The prophet proclaims God's promise to bring encouragement to the people. The words of the prophet are meant as a rallying cry, an energizing force, an empowering message. God loves you amid your trauma and grief. God will continue to give you life and hope.

Isaiah 54:9-10 sums up this message of hope. "This is like the days of Noah to me: Just as I swore that the waters of Noah would never again go over the earth, so I have sworn that I will not be angry with you and will not rebuke you. For the mountains may depart and the hill be removed, but my steadfast love shall not depart from you, and my covenant of peace shall not be removed, says the Lord, who has compassion on you."

## Questions for Thought and Discussion

1. What valid role do human institutions play in the life of faith? How might the types of problems that plagued ancient Israel's religious and political institutions (injustice, idolatry, etc.) be avoided or overcome in our day?

2. What do you understand to be the bases for the words of hope proclaimed in Isaiah? Are these relevant as bases for *our* hope?

3. God's promise to Abraham and Sarah serves as one source for encouragement in Isaiah 51. How might we understand it as a source for encouragement for us today?

4. Can you think of experiences in your own life or others' where shattering loss gave birth to hope? How do you understand such experiences?

5. What seems most significant to you in the point that God's words of hope in Isaiah were addressed to people who had been unfaithful?

## Further Reading

On the message of hope in Isaiah 40–55, see Paul Hanson, *Isaiah 40–66*; George A. F. Knight, *Servant Theology: Isaiah 40–55*; and Claus Westermann, *Isaiah 40–66*. On theme of hope in exile more generally, see Ralph W. Klein, *Israel in Exile: A Theological Interpretation*.

# 7

# The Message
# of the Old Testament

$M$Y SUMMARY OF SOME OF THE MAIN IDEAS in the Old Testament reflects my belief that we can find in the Old Testament a thread or trajectory or basic plot line that points forward to Jesus and the Christian heritage.

Let me summarize seven main aspects of this story line.

(1) *Creation.* What is, is good, created good by a loving God who is committed to genuine relationship of freedom with humankind.

(2) *Disruption.* The breaking of the original harmony happens when Adam and Eve reject the limitations that God has placed on them. With their rebellion, sin enters into the world. We then see a spiral of violence—their son Cain murders his brother Abel, the Flood of Noah, the building of the Tower of Babel. However, God remains committed to relationship with human beings. We see this commitment in the rainbow God gives after the Flood.

(3) *God's healing strategy.* This strategy begins with the calling of Abraham and Sarah to found a community of faith. God promises this community that it will serve as a blessing for all the families of the earth.

(4) *Exodus.* God's healing strategy continues by God liberating Abraham's descendants from slavery in Egypt. This exodus frees the people to enter the Promised Land, which they are given

so they may establish their community. In leaving Egypt, they reject the values of Egypt.

(5) *Nationhood.* Israel's history as a nation-state involves mixed results in relation to God's will for them. The people of Israel choose not to live with God as their king. They need a human king. King David becomes Israel's greatest king—and leaves a mixed legacy. In many ways he is faithful—"a person after God's heart." However, King David sins grievously against God and his people when he commits adultery with Bathsheba and, in effect, murders Bathsheba's husband.

David's son, Solomon, decisively moves the institution of human kingship in the direction of authoritarianism. The movement of Israel away from the vision of Moses continues under kings such as King Ahab—and includes becoming a society more and more like that of Egypt.

(6) *Prophetic Witness.* God remains involved with the rebellious Hebrews. God's commitment is expressed by the great prophets. The prophets keep alive the ideals of peace (shalom), justice, compassion for the weak and needy, and accountability to God. The prophets challenge corrupt kings (Elijah), critique injustice (Amos), and speak of God's ongoing love (Hosea).

(7) *Exile.* The great Babylonian empire conquers Egypt. Some see this as the judgment of God due to their disobedience to God's will. However, even in the context of judgment and exile from the Israelite's homeland, God still speaks words of hope to people of faith, pointing forward to a new expression of God's healing strategy (which Christians understand to be fulfilled in the coming of Jesus).

Before we go on with the biblical story and consider Jesus, however, more reflection on the God of the Old Testament is in order. I want to summarize some of the Old Testament's main points about God.

The God of the Old Testament is *with* God's people and *for* God's people. This is another way of speaking about God being

a covenant-making, covenant-keeping God. God makes promises. God makes agreements with human beings. God is committed to this relationship and desires that humans be committed to
this relationship also.

This is God's central attribute—not first of all that God is
all-knowing, never-changing, judgmental, or all-powerful.
Rather, first of all God *relates* to the community of God's people
and to creation as a faithful covenant-keeper, as a promise-ful-
filler, as a relationship-sustainer. God as the one who remains
faithful to God's covenants is the core reality or theme of God's
healing strategy.

How does thinking of God as first of all covenant-keeper
affect our understanding of God's response to human disobedience? We see that God lets humans suffer the consequences of sin
in the hope that we will eventually return to God. God does not
want to punish as an end in itself. The judgment that God does
exercise is not simply to inflict pain; rather, it is to lead to life.
God's mercy, in the end, is stronger than God's anger.

We might see four different dimensions that characterize the
Old Testament portrayal of God as covenant-keeper. (1) God
creates a people. (2) God acts on behalf of this people. (3) God
abides with this people. (4) God strengthens this people.

(1) The first dimension is that *God creates a people*. God as
covenant-keeper creates a people who did not previously exist
and gives them well-being when they had none.

We have discussed the story of the calling of Abraham and
Sarah in Genesis 12. They are childless and because of Sarah's
barrenness have no hope for children. However, God is not con-
fined by this barrenness. God gives them a future. God gives
them children. God creates something new, a people meant to
know God in a special way and also help others come to know
God. Abraham and Sarah are the spiritual ancestors of all Christians—the first members of the community of faith whose heritage extends down to the present.

We also see God's covenant-making when the children of Israel are in slavery in Egypt. They are facing this situation several generations after Abraham, but their existence, as a people, is in jeopardy. The life is slowly being ground out of them, and they cry out to God.

God sees their affliction. God hears their cry. God knows their sufferings. And God comes down to deliver them (Exod. 3:7-8). God remembers the promise to Abraham. God remains faithful to that covenant. God brings possibilities for well-being for God's people.

(2) The second dimension is that *God acts*. God as covenant-keeper acts on behalf of these people to bring them liberation from slavery. God fights for them.

The core story of salvation in the Old Testament, the exodus, tells of God saving God's people by acting on their behalf to free them. God fights for those who cannot defend themselves.

This war language ("the Lord will fight for you") is uncomfortable for many Christians. The point that God *acts* on behalf of his people to bring them salvation is important, even if we are uncomfortable with the idea that this means war and people being killed. However, the New Testament also uses similar language about Jesus. He defeated the powers of sin and death. He won the victory for us. He acted on our behalf to liberate us from our slavery to those powers of sin and death. One term used for what Jesus did to bring salvation is "spiritual warfare."

In some sense, at least, we can say that the portrayal of God's acts to save Israel pre-figure what Jesus did to save all humanity. The big difference—a crucial difference—is that Jesus defeated the spiritual powers of evil. He did not wage war against human beings. In fact, Jesus refused the option of calling down legions of angels to do battle with the soldiers who came to arrest and crucify him.

The context of God's war-like actions changes from focusing on people (the Egyptians) to focusing on the spiritual forces which enslave such people as the Egyptians. In both cases, however, the key point is that God is covenant-keeper who acts to bring salvation.

(3) The third dimension is that *God abides*. God as covenant-keeper is an abiding presence with God's people.

This dimension especially has to do with the worship life of God's people. In genuine worship, God's people are assured a free, safe space in which to receive joyous life. They are assured a sanctuary where worth is guaranteed and dignity protected.

Especially the prophets point out dangers with this dimension. Active religiosity and ritual can sometimes go on even while the people live lives of injustice and exploitation. Also, the faith community can be tempted to think God is present only in worship and not in the rest of life.

However, in such cases the worship is not authentic. It is self-worship, not worship of God. God's presence abides—but public worship, to be a place where that presence is real for the people, must happen in the context of general faithfulness in other areas of life.

(4) The fourth dimension is that *God strengthens*. God as covenant-keeper strengthens God's people in their distress. God strengthens the people when they feel most hopeless. We see this in a word from God throughout the Old Testament—"fear not." Fear not, I have not abandoned you even when things seem hard and unbearable, even when you are terrified.

This word from God carried special weight toward the end of the Old Testament story. We discussed the kings and their corruption. Eventually, the Israelite nation-state was wiped out. Many of the Israelites were taken into exile. They despaired about their future. Was God's plan destroyed? Was this people of God going to come to an end?

The prophet said no—God still has a future for you. "Fear not, for I have redeemed you; I have called you by name, you are mine. When you pass through the waters, I will be with you"

(Isa. 43:1-2). God strengthened the exiles and helped them to continue in the faith, even in their hard times.

These four dimensions of God as covenant-keeper all have to do with God's most unique and special characteristic: that God is *for* God's people; that God is *with* God's people. There is a word which means "God with us"—*Emmanuel*. This is a word the Bible uses of Jesus. Emmanuel—God with us. Jesus is the supreme expression of God as covenant-keeper. God is with us in the flesh. God is for us in bringing salvation to the whole earth.

The Old Testament God is most of all a covenant-keeper. God's original covenant with Abraham included the promise that God would bless all the families of the earth through Abraham's descendants. The Old Testament tells the story of those descendants. Often, as we have discussed, they were anything but a blessing. And at times the light of that old promise to Abraham flickered low. However, the light does stay alive. Abraham's descendants survive as a people. And some at least remember that old promise.

Mary, the mother of Jesus, remembers. She responds to being told that she will be the mother of God's Son by singing a song of praise: "God has helped God's servant Israel, in remembrance of God's mercy, according to the promise God made to our ancestors, to Abraham and to God's descendants forever" (Luke 1:54-55). The coming of Jesus is God keeping God's promise—God acting as covenant-keeper.

## Questions for Thought and Discussion

1. After revisiting the Old Testament with the help of this book, how would you characterize its core message? Do you now agree that the Old Testament communicates a message about God's mercy and love?

2. Do you find the portrayal of God in the Old Testament attractive or unattractive? In continuity with the New Testament or in fundamental tension with it?

3. What to you is of central importance in the affirmation of God as "covenant-keeper"?

4. How do you understand the Old Testament's war language? What is its relevance for our faith? How (if at all) does it fit with Jesus' life and teachings? What might be some tensions with Jesus' way?

## Further Reading

This chapter basically follows Walter Brueggemann's outline of the Old Testament's core message in *The Bible Makes Sense*. Other studies which have had an influence include Millard Lind, *Yahweh is a Warrior*; Walter Brueggemann, *The Theology of the Old Testament*; Brueggemann, *Interpretation and Obedience*; Brueggemann, *A Social Reading of the Old Testament*; Paul Hanson, *A People Called*; George Mendenhall, *The Tenth Generation*; Gabriel Josipovici, *The Book of God*; and Bruce Birch, *Let Justice Roll Down*.

# 8

# Jesus and the Liberating Kingdom of God (Mark 1:1–8:30)

WITH JESUS, WE DO NOT BEGIN OUT of nothing. Jesus ministers as part of the entire biblical story of God's healing strategy. Historically, he is part of the same narrative, the same peoplehood, as the people of the Old Testament. Theologically and ethically he is also closely related to what we have seen, especially to ancient Israel's prophetic tradition.

We may identify several continuities from the Old Testament to Jesus.

(1) As has been true since the time of Jeremiah, now six hundred years later Israel is still dominated by a large empire. In Jeremiah's time it was Babylon, followed by Persia, then Greece. Finally, about one hundred years before Jesus began his public ministry, the Roman Empire took control of Palestine. Israel existed, in many ways, as part of a Roman colony. The people were ruled by a client king in Galilee (Herod Antipas, servant of the Romans) and a Roman governor in Judea (Pontius Pilate).

(2) As was true in the Book of Daniel in the second century BC, now still 200 years later revolution was in the air. Jesus' society was in turmoil, revolutionary sentiment led by radicals later known as Zealots were stirring up opposition to Rome. This was to erupt into a full-scale revolution in the years 66 to 70 AD

(about thirty years after Jesus' death). At that time, the Romans were driven out of Jerusalem, but they then returned in force and destroyed the Jewish temple.

(3) As with Amos, now still 800 years later economic injustice was widespread. Also present were poverty, landlessness, and a large disinherited peasant class. The inheritance regulations, which Elijah had defended in the time of King Ahab, were long gone. Religion was generally a force that supported this unjust status quo, as it had been in the time of Solomon and in the generations following Solomon.

(4) Jesus' basic message echoed many prophetic themes from the Old Testament. Our loving, merciful, creative God gives life as a gift. God also expects that those who know God's mercy share it with others. Jesus, like the prophets, offered a critique of power politics, of trusting in weapons of war, of oppression, of people seeking wealth and worldly success above all else. Jesus continued the Old Testament understanding of God's healing strategy through the calling of a people who would know God and who would share that knowledge with others—blessing all the families of the earth.

## Jesus Shows the Kingdom as Present

The Gospels do not say much about Jesus' life before he began his public ministry. The Gospel of Mark says the least. It begins with Jesus as an *adult*, meeting John the Baptist.

Jesus, it appears, sensed the time was drawing near for him to carry out his destiny. So he left the populated areas and went to the wilderness. That is where he came into contact with a wild-eyed Jewish prophet named John the Baptist. John was preaching a harsh message: Repent of your sins or you will suffer terrible consequences. John's passion and message that a crisis was at hand drew a number of followers to him. To those he offered the ritual of baptism as a sign of the cleansing work of God and of the baptized person's commitment to follow God's ways.

Jesus was impressed with John's preaching and took the step of receiving John's baptism. We are not told exactly why—perhaps mostly as a clear statement of submission to God's will for his life, an expression of his commitment to devote his life to serving God by spreading the good news of God's salvation.

God approved Jesus' baptism. As Jesus came out of the baptismal waters, says Mark 1:10-11, "he saw the heavens torn apart and the Spirit descending like a dove on him. And a voice came from heaven, 'You are my Son, the Beloved; with you I am well pleased.'"

The precise significance of Jesus' baptism is not spelled out. Yet God's statement echoes Psalm 2, a royal psalm used at the inauguration of a king, and Isaiah 42, which highlights the suffering servant. Thus God appears here to fold king and suffering servant into one. Clearly this is a turning point for Jesus. With a new sense of God's empowerment, he is ready to begin his ministry. He will not continue to work with John the Baptist. Though John is making a valuable contribution, Jesus has a more positive message than "turn or burn."

Before Jesus is ready to proclaim his positive message, however, he moves even deeper into the wilderness. Here he undergoes a time of preparation, of deep soul-searching, deep God-searching. After forty days of fasting, Jesus is tempted by Satan. In facing these genuine temptations at this time, Jesus experiences a foretaste of what he will struggle with the rest of his life.

How will he respond to brokenness in the world most effectively? How will he do the most good? How will he be God's beloved Son, as God pronounced him at baptism?

According to the Gospels of Matthew and Luke, which go into more detail than Mark, Satan offers Jesus three options. Each is a shortcut for bringing salvation. Jesus says no to these shortcuts. He will trust in God's ways.

The core temptation for Jesus, as I understand it, is this: Jesus is being tempted to invite God to step in and fix whatever is wrong with the world. The shortcuts Satan offers Jesus for bringing salvation will not respect human freedom.

Jesus does not stay in the wilderness. One response to these temptations would have been to stay. For instance, Jesus could have founded a monastery. Jesus' place, however, is with his people. So he returns to the reality of life in Galilee, his home area. Here he will again face the brokenness of the world.

In Mark, Jesus starts with a simple proclamation. "The time is fulfilled, and the kingdom of God is at hand; repent and believe in the good news" (1:15). These brief words are both Jesus' opening statement and summarize what Jesus is about. What is Jesus saying here? The kingdom is at hand. Repent and believe the good news. But what does Jesus mean by "kingdom of God"?

(1) The kingdom has to do with *seeing* that God is present in the world right now and wants people to follow God right now. Jesus does not speak of the kingdom in terms of thrones, courtiers, heavenly choirs, or multitudes with chariots, swords, or spears. Rather, Jesus speaks of the kingdom in terms of everyday life. The kingdom of God is like a field, a vineyard, a tiny seed, the fish, the cook. It is the home of the humble and trusting and the poor—more so than the rich and powerful.

Look around. The kingdom is at hand wherever people have eyes to see, and wherever people live with God as their ruler.

(2) The second point about Jesus' understanding of the kingdom is this: Jesus *reminds* people what God is like. Jesus proclaims that the kingdom "is at hand." This is a reminder of what the Bible from Genesis onward affirms. Jesus reminds his listeners that God is the loving creator and sustainer for us all and that God's world is abundant in resources of mercy and caring, just as it is abundant in physical resources of beauty and food and the other goods we need.

The arrival of the kingdom in the proclamation and person of Jesus is *not* God's return to the world after a long absence. Instead, it is the coming of a God-inspired prophet to remind believers, to remind those with ears to hear: God has always been present. All you need is faith, all you need are eyes to see. With trust in God, the way toward abundant living can again be discovered. The arrival of the kingdom with Jesus is the arrival of a person specially blessed and called by God to show this way toward abundant living.

Jesus brings to light in a fresh way what has always been the case but what we continually forget. Mercy and generosity are the ways of God and are the paths toward human flourishing. We may be merciful and generous with one another because that is what God offers us.

Jesus is saying that God's plan in calling Abraham and Sarah and in liberating the children of Israel from slavery in Egypt remains in effect. God calls for a people to live with God as their only king and by doing so to bless all the families of the earth.

The kingdom Jesus proclaims first of all has to do with being aware that God is *present*. Look and see. God's love and mercy are the central truths in the universe. Second, Jesus *reminds* his listeners that this is the way God has always been and will continue to be.

(3) But there remains a third point to make about the kingdom. Jesus does have a hard edge to his message of the kingdom. He calls for *repentance*. Jesus echoes the terminology of John the Baptist: "Repent." However, Jesus' meaning is different. John has commanded repentance to avoid the wrath to come. Turn or burn. Jesus says, Repent because of God's good news. To oversimplify, John offers a stick; Jesus dangles a carrot. John says, prove you mean it by submitting to my baptism. Jesus simply invites belief in the good news. Jesus doesn't require a ritual. Jesus asks only for trust.

Of course, Jesus does assume, as his teachings show, that such trust makes for changed lives which yield genuine fruit. Such trust leads to concrete expressions of love which affect other people and the world.

Nevertheless, in contrast to the repentance John demands, the repentance Jesus asks for is not generated by fear. The repentance Jesus asks for is a change in thinking. Repent of your pride and arrogance, your hatred toward others, your selfishness—and turn toward humility, love, and generosity.

To summarize: First, Jesus' proclamation of the kingdom speaks to a way of seeing, an awareness of God present as ruler in all areas of life. Second, Jesus' proclamation of the kingdom reminds his listeners of what Israel has always believed about God. God is a covenant-keeping God. Third, Jesus calls on his listeners to repent of misplaced priorities, of being closed-off to God, and to believe the good news of God's mercy and love.

## Jesus' Mighty Works

After proclaiming the good news that the kingdom is at hand, Jesus gives signs to show that this is indeed true. Jesus shows mercy in concrete ways—healing diseases, casting out demons, forgiving sins, welcoming people seen to be unclean by the religious authorities.

We can look at this aspect of Jesus' ministry in three stages: (1) Jesus' initial expression of healing power; (2) problems which arise with regard to his mighty works; (3) a change in Jesus' focus *away* from doing mighty works.

From the beginning, Jesus draws great crowds. As he proclaims the nearness of the kingdom, Jesus cures "many . . . sick with various diseases, and cast[s] out many demons" (Mark 1:33). As we might expect, in so doing Jesus quickly becomes well-known. We read in Mark 3:7-8 that "a great multitude . . . followed him [as he traveled about] hearing all that he was doing, they came to him in great numbers from [miles around]." Many of those who come are "afflicted with various pains, demoniacs, epileptics, and paralytics," and Jesus cures them (Matt. 4:24).

We have here a moving picture of a Jesus who offers spontaneous compassion. He faces close up and first hand the brokenness of his world. And he *responds*. In these early stories of Jesus' healings and exorcisms, we see him putting flesh to the pronouncement that the kingdom of God is at hand.

The presence of the kingdom means freedom from the power of disease, freedom from the power of demonic oppression, freedom from the power of being outcast from a society that blamed the victims and declared them unclean. In God's abundance, we see unconditional acceptance of these so-called unclean and outcasts and demon-possessed. Jesus doesn't ask many questions. Rather, he heals the needy. He simply shows that God's love is genuine and powerful.

However, we do not have to read far into the story to begin to see shadows. Jesus' healing will not simply bring about heaven on earth. John's Gospel states the concern clearly. "Many believed in Jesus' name because they saw the signs that [Jesus] was doing. But Jesus on his part would not entrust himself to them, because he knew all people" (John 2:23-24). All the Gospels raise this issue: Are the people following Jesus only as one who does wonders? Do they genuinely want to know God?

From the start Jesus combines his teaching with his healings and exorcisms. We read in Matthew 4 of the crowds following Jesus. As we read on into Matthew 5 we are told, "When Jesus saw the crowds, he went up to the mountain; and after he sat down, his disciples came to him. Then he began to speak, and taught them" (5:1-2). What follows is Jesus' Sermon on the Mount. Jesus combines teaching with healing activity. He is never only a teacher. Nor is he ever only a miracle-worker. Jesus' message is that God is abundant in compassion and caring. Jesus teaches this—and showed it.

Ultimately, though, dangers and problems arise in relation to Jesus' healing activities. We see this also in John's Gospel. Jesus has drawn a huge crowd, and he sees that they are hungry. He feeds them, 5,000 strong. "When the people saw the sign that he had done, they began to say, 'This is indeed the prophet who is to come into the world.' When Jesus realized that they were about to come and take him by force to make him king, he withdrew again to the mountain by himself" (John 6:14-15).

However, Jesus does not want to be a king like the nations had. He does not want to follow in the footsteps of Old Testament kingship and be corrupted by earthly power and wealth.

Yet much of the following Jesus attracts through his miracles is of this sort. If not all are interested in making him king by force, most at least are interested in following Jesus as a wonder worker. They are not people he can trust himself to. They misunderstand his message.

Jesus constantly faces the temptation of placing too high a priority on short-term effectiveness. Would it not be most *effective* for Jesus simply to step up his campaign of miracles, healings, exorcisms, providing food, raising from the dead? He is gathering crowds from all over. He is face-to-face with profound brokenness and need. And he has the means, he has the resources at his disposal, to intervene directly—to *fix* the world.

However, to try to fix all the world's problems in this way is to take a short cut. Although Jesus is tempted to take the shortcut, he knows that what is needed is a deeper, more long-term change in people's hearts.

## Jesus' Teaching

If I were to characterize Jesus' teaching in a sentence, it is that Jesus' teachings address his listeners' hearts. The main point of Jesus' teachings is to touch our hearts, to help us to see, to help us know ourselves, especially to help us know God and God's will for our lives.

We see Jesus' style of teaching most clearly in his use of parables. To say that Jesus taught in parables means, simply, that he used stories.

These stories were brief, sometimes only a sentence or two, never more than what our Bibles measure as fifteen to twenty verses. They are full of illustrations, comparisons, word pictures. The kingdom of God is like a mustard seed, or like yeast, or like the shepherd looking for lost sheep. Love is like the Samaritan merchant helping the highway-robbed and beaten traveler on the Jericho Road. God's mercy is like the father welcoming back his prodigal son.

Often parables are paradoxical. Almost always they operate with several layers of meaning. The parable of the Good Samaritan in Luke tells a simple story of a travelling merchant being nice to someone who had been beaten and robbed. Then we find out that Samaritans and Jews were enemies. And the victim is a Jew. *Jewish* religious leaders walked by him and did not stop as he lay bleeding because blood is unclean. The man who does stop is a Samaritan. So, the story makes a deeper point. We hear of surprising acts of caring. Then we notice the story is introduced by an interchange where Jesus is asked, "Who is my neighbor?" So it is not just an uplifting anecdote but a story which illustrates the meaning of neighborliness, a story which contains barbs aimed at religious exclusiveness, excess piety, too much defining of who's clean and unclean and not enough on freely caring for those in need.

That Jesus taught in parables may give clues to his concerns. A few characteristics of his parable style deserve mention.

First, Jesus' parables are down-to-earth. They have to do with practical, everyday life. Second, Jesus' parables reflect a positive view of life, a respectful and hopeful view, of life in this world and of human possibilities. Third, Jesus' parables often challenge our expectations.

(1) *Jesus' parables are down-to-earth.* The earthiness of Jesus' parables is one of their main characteristics. Jesus celebrates people's everyday existence. *Here* is precisely where God's grace enters our lives. God expresses God's love in the everyday world.

In looking at a list of Jesus' parables, it is striking how almost every one has to do with everyday situations. You have the shepherd searching for lost sheep. The woman hunts madly for a lost coin. We read of the controversy over the workers in the vineyard all getting paid the same, even though some worked more hours than others. We hear about people owing money, people building barns and towers, weddings, people fishing and planting and harvesting grain.

Jesus uses earthy reality as his source of teaching about God because that is how people best know God. For Jesus, God is not best known primarily in mystical contemplation, abstract theologizing, nor sacred, set-apart worship. God is known in day-to-day human work and social interaction and family relationships and moving about from here to there. All of life is a whole.

(2) *Jesus' parables reflect a positive view of life.* They reflect an ultimately positive view of human beings. Jesus rejects the image of the world as merely a hard place, so dominated by evil that the good can only prevail through heroic efforts on the part of a few righteous people. Any number of unlikely persons—Samaritans, Gentile kings—take extraordinary actions for good in these stories. They show something of God's involvement in life, and that life is good.

I have mentioned the Samaritan merchant who unexpectedly helped the beaten traveler. We also have the story of the rich man who forgives his unjust manager (Luke 16:1-9), and at the other extreme the rich man who ignores the righteous beggar Lazarus (Luke 16:19-31). These stories show that all kinds of people are capable of responding to God. All kinds of people can act creatively and faithfully—from one of the hated Samaritans to a rich capitalist to a homeless beggar.

Jesus does picture some negative human behavior, but overall we do not find in his parables pessimism about the human condition. To the contrary, Jesus pictures God as making room for people to respond positively to God's grace. Many of the people who populate these stories are not wretched sinners or at least can choose not to be. They are managers who respond creatively to a boss's call for accountability. They are prodigal sons coming to themselves and returning home to throw themselves at their fathers' mercy. They are bridesmaids who think ahead to take enough oil for their lamps so they will have light if the bridegroom is delayed. They are people given talents who invest them wisely.

We often do have contrasts—the bridesmaids who do not bring oil, the one person who does not invest his talent. But the emphasis is on people who are creative and capable of responding with compassion and imagination. Such responses are not automatic. Jesus is not naive. He does challenge people, though, to respond as he knows we are capable of responding. We *are* capable of compassion and imagination. All we need are eyes that see and hearts that trust that the kingdom of God is indeed among us.

(3) *Jesus' parables often challenge our expectations.* Again we see this in the famous Good Samaritan parable. This is hard for us fully to relate to because we are so familiar with the story. However, Jesus shocked his first listeners by making the one who stops a Samaritan. He presents an outsider showing what neighborliness is like.

This confounding of expectations evokes that famous Old Testament parable the prophet Nathan tells King David. He strings David along with his story of how the rich person had taken the poor person's last sheep. Then comes the twist—"That robber is you, David!" Jesus often does that kind of thing, giving the story a surprising outcome—sometimes in the course of the story, such as the Good Samaritan, sometimes simply in the imagery he uses.

The parable of the mustard seed shows this. "The kingdom of God is like a mustard seed that someone took and sowed in his field; it is the smallest of all the seeds, but when it has grown it is the greatest of shrubs and becomes a tree, so that the birds of the air come and make nests in its branches" (Mark 4:31-32).

We might miss the irony in this parable. The image of the birds nesting is a messianic one from the Old Testament. In Ezekiel, we read of God's promise in the age to come to plant a great cedar in Israel which will host winged creatures of every kind. Later, this image is used in Daniel, where we read that "the birds of the air nested in its branches," the great tree (Dan. 4:12).

The prophetic image of great cedars had comforted ancient Israel in hard times. This image promises future greatness—a hope still current in Jesus' time. But Jesus offers something different. Instead of great cedars you get mustard bushes. Cedars had to be imported from Lebanon. They were the stuff of the high and mighty, kings and great warriors. Mustard bushes grew everywhere. Anyone could grow one.

Jesus says "kingdom of God" and people think great, new, political revolution, big transformations. However, Jesus' image challenges their expectations. In effect, he says, do not look for the influx of great cedars from the outside. Do not expect the kingdom of God to be something radically different or awe-inspiring or all-powerful. The kingdom is at-hand already. We see it in the mustard bush. After all, a healthy mustard bush serves just fine as a nesting home for the birds. God's rule does not have to appear in the grandiose; a mustard seed growing into a mustard bush will do just as well. You can live the way of the kingdom right now, in *this* life.

Jesus was a powerful teacher. He was down to earth. He taught a positive view of life. He challenged people's expectations. Jesus presented God's kingdom as present by using vivid, earthy, everyday imagery. God is here in real life. Open your hearts to God.

Jesus called on his listeners to respond—and expected that they would.

Jesus' ministry—mighty works of healing, powerful teaching, mercy, and compassion—led, shockingly enough, to conflict. In fact, his way of ministering led to him losing his life.

## Questions for Thought and Discussion

1. How do you respond to the argument that Jesus is in basic *continuity* with the Old Testament? What do you think the *discontinuities* are? How do you hold the continuities and discontinuities together?

2. What is the significance of taking seriously the fact that the Palestine of Jesus' day was ruled by the Roman empire?

3. How do you understand these two key events at the beginning of Jesus' ministry: his baptism and his temptations in the wilderness? What significance do they have for the actions and events that follow in his life?

4. What do you think is more important in Jesus' use of the phrase *kingdom of God*? What does his use of this metaphor tell us about God and God's involvement with human beings?

5. Why did Jesus perform miracles of healing? What do these tell us about his ministry? What relevance do the stories of Jesus' miracles have for us?

6. Why would people have been hostile to Jesus? If he were among us today, where do you think he would meet with the most hostility? Why?

7. Which of Jesus' parables are your favorites? What about them do you like? Why do *you* think Jesus taught with parables?

## Further Reading

See the references following chapter 9 below.

# 9

# The Cost of Faithfulness to God (Mark 8:31–16:8)

*T*HE GOSPEL OF MARK TELLS US about Jesus doing mighty deeds. He proclaims the presence of God's kingdom. He shows the power of the kingdom with his healings, his miracles, his casting out demons. He teaches with authority and unmatched insight. He calls people to follow him and forms a community of followers—the core being the twelve disciples.

## The Cost of Faithfulness

However, Jesus' message is not simply, "Let the good times roll!" He faces increased opposition from various people. He realizes that living out his message will require some suffering. This becomes clear in the passage that is at the center of the gospel of Mark, 8:27-38. Jesus has just cured a blind man; he and the disciples are on the road.

Jesus asks the disciples, "'Who do the people say that I am?' And they answered him, 'John the Baptist; and others, Elijah; and still others, one of the prophets.' He asked them, 'But who do you say that I am?' Peter answered him, 'You are the Messiah.'"

Jesus accepts Peter's answer but then begins "to teach them that the Son of man must undergo great suffering, and be rejected by the elders, the chief priests, and the scribes, and be killed, and after three days rise again. He said all this quite openly. And Peter took him aside and began to rebuke him. But turning and looking at his disciples, [Jesus] rebuked Peter and said, 'Get behind me, Satan! For you are setting your mind not on divine things but on human things.'"

Jesus rebukes Peter because Peter fails to understand what type of Messiah Jesus is. Jesus is not a mighty king who will never face suffering. Jesus will be a Messiah who brings salvation through his death. Peter cannot understand that, at least not yet.

Jesus also connects the suffering he himself must face with the suffering his followers will face. "If any want to become my followers, let them deny themselves and take up their cross and follow me. For those who want to save their life will lose it, and those who lose their life for my sake, and for the sake of the gospel, will save it" (Mark 8:34-35).

Jesus realizes he must go to Jerusalem to suffer, even to die. Six days later, Jesus takes Peter, John, and James with him to the mountain to pray. There Jesus meets Moses and Elijah and talks with them about his going to Jerusalem to face suffering and death. This "transfiguration" is followed by God's voice repeating the words from Jesus' baptism, "this is my beloved son," and adding, "listen to him!" (Mark 9:7).

Jesus met with great success in the early days of his public ministry as he powerfully expressed the abundance of God's kingdom. He gained wide notice as a healer, a popular preacher, and teacher. It seemed he was about to take the world by storm—and usher in the kingdom with great acclaim.

But now it is clear that Jesus is up against some mighty powers of resistance. One source is the elite, the most powerful people in that society. These include the Sadducees (the Jewish religious leaders, those who run the temple) and the Herodians (associates of King Herod). These people oppose any renewal movement that threatens their dominant role.

The second source of opposition is surely more discouraging for Jesus: the Pharisees. These are people who—like him—seek change and renewal. In the Gospels, often the Pharisees are Jesus' bitterest enemies. Yet they have many of the same goals, many of the same criticisms of the way things are, many of the same hopes for renewal. Often the people with the most in common prove the most antagonistic toward each other. Their few differences become crucial.

Jesus and the Pharisees, though sharing many values, propose significantly different approaches to renewal. The Pharisees focus on more rigorous adherence to the law codes, stricter boundary lines for who is in and who is out. Jesus, in contrast, turns current practices regarding the law on their heads—kindness, openness to outsiders, mercy not sacrifice, unconditional forgiveness matter most. Rather than set more strict boundary lines, Jesus acts to transcend boundary lines. Jesus welcomes unclean outsiders to God's kingdom just as they are. Simply repent and believe the good news of the abundance of God's mercy.

So Jesus soon faces bitter opposition. It is clear he will not simply bring about widespread renewal and cultural revolution. In fact, he is likely soon to face death.

Through his time of listening to God in prayer, through his encounter with Moses and Elijah on the mount of transfiguration (Mk. 9:2-8), Jesus is ready to continue his faithfulness to God's message of the presence of the kingdom—even as this will mean suffering and death. Jesus is empowered to continue his chosen path as God's son.

After this prayer interlude, in the second half of Mark's Gospel the tenor of Jesus' teaching and actions changes. His words become darker. Jesus now focuses on helping his followers to understand the cost of genuinely living for God's ways.

So at this stage Jesus takes up his cross. He has come to realize that following his heart, following the way he knows is the truth, will be costly. Jesus knows he will walk into the teeth of a vicious storm as he continues his ministry, especially as he heads for the political and religious center of his world, Jerusalem.

Jesus begins to prepare his followers to travel the same path. He teaches about discipleship. He prepares his followers for similar fates. As he takes up his cross, he challenges his followers to do likewise.

In the materials we have considered so far in looking at Jesus' life, we have seen many attractive things. Jesus heals. Jesus proclaims God's merciful kingdom. Jesus openly welcomes all kinds of riffraff to be a part of this kingdom. Now we come to a turning point—not that these attractive things are not true and not that they are not central to what Jesus was about. They are true. They are central. But the turning point is the realization that such a way of being—merciful, open, free, generous—can be quite costly. There are forces around which do not like openness and mercy, and, in fact are threatened by openness and mercy.

Jesus will be walking into a vicious storm as he continues his ministry, especially as he heads for the political and religious center of his world, Jerusalem. Nevertheless, Jesus turns his face toward Jerusalem. He accepts that the coming suffering is for the sake of God's healing strategy. Jesus will suffer because his kind of goodness and faithfulness is not acceptable to the leaders (political and religious) in his society.

Jesus realizes that only his willingness to die can make God's salvation known. Jesus will not fight back. He will rely on God to vindicate him. Jesus teaches his followers that they too must be willing to take up their crosses. He challenges them to remain committed to love and mercy even when it is rejected, even when such commitment leads to suffering.

## Jesus' Death

From Mark 8 on, the Gospel writer focuses on the coming death of Jesus. Jewish society around Jerusalem in Jesus' time centers around two power structures: the *religious* power structure around the Jewish temple, and the *political* power structure. These power structures combine to kill Jesus.

The story of Jesus' life moves toward its climax in Mark 11, when Jesus arrives in Jerusalem to face his final week, the so-called "triumphal entry." Jesus enters Jerusalem. Many people spread palm branches before him and shout "Hosanna!"

Then one of the first things that happens after Jesus gets to Jerusalem underscores his conflict with the religious leaders. This conflict has been brewing throughout the story. In his preaching and practicing the presence of God's merciful kingdom for all people, right now, Jesus has in effect performed an end run around the religious institutions. He has acted and taught in ways that made clear he has low regard for those institutions. Instead of being instruments of God's mercy, they are *perverting* mercy for the sake of rituals and rules. So Jesus expresses God's mercy outside the authorized channels.

When Jesus cleanses the temple shortly after he arrives in Jerusalem this conflict comes to a head. He drives out the money changers and merchants. These people were making a living from pilgrims who came to worship at the temple. The money changers charged the pilgrims a fee to trade the pilgrims' foreign currency into local money usable in the temple. And others were making a living by selling at huge profit small animals suitable for sacrifice in the temple to these same pilgrims. The whole worship process had become commercialized and exclusive.

Jesus challenges these practices. Jesus wants to show that all people can know God directly, through faith. They do not need to buy animals. Jesus strongly opposes using people's desire to know God as a way to make money.

Jesus' confrontation symbolically shows his disdain for the entire corrupt religious system. In response, the religious leaders, according to Mark's Gospel, begin to look "for a way to kill Jesus" (Mark 11:18). The religious leaders cannot accept Jesus' critique of their corruption. He threatens their power and they cannot stand for it. Thus within a few days, in cooperation with the Roman political leaders, they do find a way to kill him.

Jesus is arrested. He first goes before the religious leaders, the Sanhedrin. He shows his disrespect for their alleged authority by refusing to answer their accusations. In effect, he shows that he rejects their authority. Jesus' authority comes directly from God. He needs no authorization from a corrupt institution to witness to God's ways and presence in the world.

Jesus challenges the way mercy is perverted by religiosity through the sacrifice system. The sacrifice system is how the institution makes salvation a scarce commodity. Salvation, access to God, is under the tight control of the hierarchy. The needed rituals are centralized in the temple. You have to pay. You have to jump through hoops.

Jesus rejects making salvation and access to God so complicated and dependent on corrupt religious institutions. Jesus rejects making salvation and access to God limited and scarce. Jesus witnesses to the abundance of God's mercy, directly available to all who repent and believe the good news.

And Jesus is killed for this. He dies not because he is a failure in his mission. He dies because he has succeeded. He dies because he has so compellingly witnessed to the abundance of salvation. The keepers of scarcity cannot stand that. So they respond with deadly force.

The second factor contributing to Jesus' death, along with his conflict with the religious leaders, is the response of the political leaders. For all the conflicts Jesus has with the religious leaders, the political leaders actually execute him. The governor, Pontius Pilate, oversees Jesus' death by crucifixion.

We can't fully know Pilate' motives. But he seems to see Jesus as an insignificant irritant and to use the religious leaders' hostility toward Jesus to manipulate them into offering the humiliating proclamation that "We have no king but Caesar!" (John 19:13).

The Gospel of John, which has the fullest account of this incident, portrays the events with heavy irony. Pilate facetiously calls Jesus "king of the Jews," but only as a means of getting the chief priests to say that they have no king but Caesar. For the gospel writer, though, Jesus is the genuine king. However, he is the king of a different sort of kingdom.

Political leaders such as Pilate are insensitive to the kind of truth Jesus stands for. Pilate, when he interrogates Jesus, asks a rhetorical question, "What is truth?" But he is not truly interested in the answer. Jesus replies, "Everyone who belongs to the truth listens to my voice." Pilate does not listen. He simply walks away. Pilate has no interest in Jesus' truth. He orders Jesus killed.

And so it happens. Jesus dies on a cross.

As Mark tells it, "When it was noon, darkness came over the whole land until three in the afternoon. At three o'clock Jesus cried out with a loud voice . . . 'My God, my God, why have you forsaken me?' . . . Then Jesus gave a loud cry and breathed his last" (Mark 15:34, 37).

The story of Jesus' death tells (1) of his challenging corrupt religious practices; (2) of the political leaders' lack of interest in Jesus' truth; and (3) of Jesus' faithfulness to the ways of love and mercy and trust in God right up to the end. Even in the face of his terrible suffering, even feeling abandoned by God, Jesus remained true.

## Jesus' Resurrection

The Gospel of Mark treats Jesus' resurrection in a very interesting way. We read of Jesus' death on the cross. One of the soldiers on the scene was moved to state, "Truly this man was God's Son!" (Mark 15:39). He recognizes Jesus' identity, but he speaks in the past tense. This man *was* God's Son. Jesus is dead.

Some of the people who loved Jesus the most, his mother and a couple of other women, also watched him die. Two days later, they go to his tomb to anoint his body, a Jewish custom. When they get there, Jesus is *gone*. A young man in white tells them that Jesus has been raised. The women are terrified and amazed. They flee the tomb and, in their fear, say nothing to anyone. This is where the gospel of Mark ends. The original version of Mark's Gospel tells nothing about the disciples seeing Jesus after he is raised. The other Gospels tell us about that.

Mark, though, leaves it open-ended. This is not because he disbelieves the disciples saw Jesus after the resurrection. He likely assumes his readers already know these stories. Mark wants to challenge his readers, though. He wants us to *think*. Fill in the final part of the story for yourselves. What do *you* have to do with the raised Jesus? How has he appeared to *you*? To what is he calling *you* in your life? Mark's ending is meant to encourage his readers ever since to ponder the meaning of Jesus' resurrection. What importance does Jesus' resurrection continue to have? What does Jesus' resurrection mean to us?

Let me offer three elements in response. (1) Jesus' resurrection shows that God vindicates Jesus' life as the way and truth. (2) Jesus' resurrection shows that God's love is stronger than death. Death cannot defeat God's purposes. Jesus lives on and promises that those who trust in him will also live on and need not fear death. (3) Jesus' resurrection keeps God's healing strategy going. It brings new hope, the possibility of life even in the face of death, even in the face of despair—just as it did with Jesus' first followers.

(1) *Jesus' resurrection vindicates his life.* Everything we believe about the truthfulness of Jesus' life would be unknown to us if he had not been raised. The resurrection tells us that God endorses the life Jesus lived—and that the powers of violence and death could not conquer such life.

Jesus was faithful to God through thick and thin. He witnessed to God's love for all kinds of people. He faced opposition from the religious leaders because he opened the way for even those people who were labeled unclean to know God's mercy. He faced opposition from the political leaders because he proclaimed that God's kingdom was more important than Caesar's kingdom. Jesus' death shows that such faithfulness to God is costly. Ultimately, though, Jesus' resurrection shows that such faithfulness is not in vain. God's mercy endures and cannot be defeated by the powers of death.

(2) *God's love is stronger than death.* The story of the cross tells that life is broken, that love can be attacked and even seemingly defeated, people can hurt others, people can be hurt. Even the best of human beings can be hurt. Even the best of human beings can be killed.

However, the continuation of the story beyond the cross affirms that Jesus lives on. The grave could not hold him. God's love is stronger than death. Jesus' resurrection is a promise that God will do away with death. We do not have to fear death even now, while it still exists. The Book of Revelation promises that in the End, after the final judgment, Death and Hades (where the dead go) will be thrown into the lake of fire and destroyed, once and for all. Jesus' resurrection tells us that God's love is more powerful than death. God's love will have the final say. Death need not be feared by those who trust in God.

(3) *Jesus' resurrection keeps God's healing strategy going.* Had Jesus remained in the grave, God's promises would not have been fulfilled. Jesus' resurrection brings new hope, even in the face of despair. God's promises will be fulfilled. This is the persevering love of God's healing strategy—the love that made the covenant with Noah, the love which called Abraham and Sarah, the love which liberated the children of Israel from slavery, the love which inspired the prophets.

Certainly Jesus' first followers felt despair when he was killed. In the dark hours before Jesus' death, all his disciples deserted Jesus. Peter the "rock" had told Jesus the night Jesus was arrested that he would *never* leave him. Jesus knew better. Three times that very night in the turmoil after Jesus was taken Peter was accused of being a follower of Jesus. Three times Peter said *No way! I don't know him.* Peter utterly failed. Then Peter despaired. The other disciples did as well. They were crushed by Jesus' death.

However, just a few short days later, their lives were turned around. Jesus is alive! Jesus' way *is* God's way. Jesus is the way, the life, and the truth. The Book of Acts tells how these despairing disciples became courageous witnesses to Jesus' way of salvation. They themselves faced persecution. One of their leaders, Stephen, like Jesus faced death. At that point, though, the Christians were no longer afraid. Jesus had shown the way. Jesus conquered death.

Peter himself was forgiven by Jesus. Peter then became one of the main spokespeople for the Christians. Never again would he deny Jesus. He now strongly affirmed that Jesus lives on, and Jesus is God's Son and the Savior for the entire world. Peter did this even in the face of great danger. He was imprisoned, threatened. The tradition of the church is that ultimately Peter too was killed for his faith. But Peter did not fear death because he knew Jesus had been raised, victorious over death.

## Questions for Thought and Discussion

1. Why would Jesus have gotten so angry with Peter when Peter challenged Jesus' talk of being killed? Why would Jesus have called Peter "Satan"? What does this episode tell us about Jesus' ministry?

2. How would you apply in your life Jesus' teaching to his followers to take up their crosses? Are there parallels between our lives and Jesus' that provide guidance?

3. What particularly about Jesus' actions and words would have been most likely to have raised the antipathy of the religious leaders? Do you see parallels in our day? What religious leaders in our world would be most likely to be angry with Jesus were he around today and over what issues?

4. What lessons for how we live are most appropriate to draw from Jesus' way of responding to those who sought to kill him?

5. Do you think of Jesus' death more in terms of him dying so that we don't have to or more in terms of him dying as a model for the fate his faithful followers may also endure?

6. How do you understand Jesus' treatment of the temple money changers and merchants? Is he violent? Who was he angry with and why? May we draw any applications for our lives from this episode?

7. How do you answer the questions implied by Mark's ending to his gospel? What do you have to do with the resurrected Jesus? How has he appeared to you? To what is he calling you in your life?

8. What to you is most important about Jesus' resurrection? What role does the resurrection play in your faith and discipleship? What are some problems that arise in thinking about Jesus' resurrection?

## Further Reading

The two books which have most shaped my thinking concerning the ministry of Jesus and the Christian vocation in general are Walter Wink, *Engaging the Powers* and John Howard Yoder, *The Politics of Jesus*.

Among the many important books about Jesus' life, these are ones which I have found particularly helpful: Marcus Borg, *Jesus: A New Vision*; James Breech, *The Silence of Jesus*; James Douglass, *The Nonviolent Coming of God*; George Edwards, *Jesus and the Politics of Violence*; Donald Goergen, *The Mission and Ministry of Jesus* and *The Death and Resurrection of Jesus*; Luise Schottroff and Wolfgang Stegemann, *Jesus and the Hope of the Poor*.

On Jesus' teaching: Michael Crosby, *Spirituality of the Beatitudes: Matthew's Challenge for the First Word*; Gene Davenport, *Into the Darkness: Discipleship in the Sermon on the Mount*; John Donahue, *The Gospel in Parable*; Athol Gill, *Life on the Road: The Gospel Basis for a Messianic Lifestyle*; Richard Hays, *The*

*Moral Vision of the New Testament*; Luke T. Johnson, *Sharing Possessions: Mandate and Symbol of Faith*; Ulrich Mauser, *The Gospel of Peace: A Scriptural Message for Today's World*; Paul Minear, *Commands of Christ: Authority and Implications*; Sharon Ringe, *Liberation and the Biblical Jubilee*; and William C. Spohn, *Go and Do Likewise: Jesus and Ethics*.

On the gospel of Mark: Morna Hooker, *The Gospel According to Saint Mark*; Werner Kelber, *Mark's Story of Jesus*; Ched Myers, *Binding the Strong Man: A Political Reading of Mark's Story of Jesus*; Pheme Perkins, "Mark" in *New Interpreters Bible*; Herman Waetjen, *A Reordering of Power: A Socio-Political Reading of Mark's Gospel*; and Lamar Williamson, *Mark*.

# 10

# The Church Expands
# (Acts 1:1–8:8)

THE GOSPELS CONTAIN THE MESSAGE of God's work for human salvation in the life, death, and resurrection of Jesus. Then, Acts tells of the working out of that initial work of salvation.

After Jesus ascends to heaven, he sends the Holy Spirit to empower his followers to spread the good news of God's healing work. Just before Jesus leaves, he tells the disciples, "You will receive power when the Holy Spirit has come upon you; and you will be my witnesses in Jerusalem, in all Judea and Samaria, and to the ends of the earth" (Acts 1:8).

The Book of Acts then tells the story of how the early Christians carried out Jesus' words—furthering God's healing strategy. A few days after Jesus' ascension, the Holy Spirit visited the disciples and other followers of Jesus in an amazingly powerful way. They then began to spread far and wide the word of God's salvation offered through Jesus.

Jesus had spoken of three stages in the spread of the gospel: (1) in Jerusalem; (2) in all Judea and Samaria (the region around Jerusalem); and (3) to the ends of the earth.

First, Jesus had said, "You will be my witnesses in Jerusalem." The first seven chapters of Acts tell of Peter's preaching in Jerusalem, the witness of many other Christians—and scores of people in Jerusalem trusting in Jesus.

Second, Jesus had said, "You will be my witnesses in all

Judea and Samaria." The apostles met with success in Jerusalem; they also met with opposition. One of their leaders, Stephen, was stoned to death. Like Jesus, these Christians had conflicts with the religious leaders who saw the Christians as rejecting standard religious procedures and threatening the status quo. Also like Jesus, the early Christians had conflicts with the political leaders who saw them threatening the social order. The Christians were violently persecuted and driven out of Jerusalem.

This was far from being a setback, however. It was like what happens when you kick a dandelion. Your violent action only spreads the seeds wider. In being driven from Jerusalem, the Christians preached the gospel in the surrounding areas—in Judea and Samaria.

Third, Jesus had said, "You will be my witnesses to the ends of the earth." The rest of Acts tells of the ever wider area reached by the gospel. Acts reaches its conclusion when, after many trials and tribulations, the Apostle Paul reaches the city of Rome, the heart of the Empire. This is likely meant to be seen as a fulfillment of Jesus' words—witnessing to the ends of the earth.

I will highlight three themes in the early chapters of Acts: (1) the outpouring of the Holy Spirit which reversed what had happened with the tower of Babel; (2) Peter's preaching of the gospel, emphasizing the centrality of Jesus' resurrection; and (3) the way in which the promise to Abraham (that his descendants would bless all the families of the earth) was carried on.

(1) Jesus promised that the Holy Spirit would come in power upon his followers. Three manifestations of the coming of the Spirit deserve particular attention.

(a) "Devout Jews from every nation under heaven" were in Jerusalem, mostly for the Jewish Feast of Weeks holiday or Pentecost, as it came to be called in reference to the fact that it was observed fifty days after Passover. When the Spirit came upon the followers of Jesus, they began to proclaim the gospel in other languages, so all these foreigners could understand.

The consequences of the Tower of Babel had been scrambled languages and inability of people to understand one another. The Holy Spirit now overturns these effects. One manifestation of the outpouring of the Holy Spirit, then, is to spread understanding. People of all languages hear and understand the gospel.

(b) A second manifestation of the Spirit is powerful, fearless proclamation. When the followers of Jesus speak in other languages, people are amazed and ask what in the world is going on. Peter—no longer afraid as he had been when Jesus was arrested—stands up and tells them. He begins by saying that the prophecy of the Old Testament prophet Joel is now fulfilled. "In the last days it will be, God declares, that I will pour out my Spirit upon all flesh" (Acts 2:17). Peter then speaks powerfully of Jesus, dead and resurrected, as the way to salvation.

(c) A third manifestation is people caring for each other's needs. The first Christians practice the justice Amos had called for. "With great power the apostles gave their testimony to the resurrection of the Lord Jesus, and great grace was upon them all. There was not a needy person among them, for as many as owned lands or houses sold them and brought the proceeds of what was sold. They laid it at the apostles' feet, and it was distributed to each as any had need" (Acts 4:33-35).

The Spirit came in power among the first Christians. This was manifested in the breaking down of language barriers, leading to fearless witnessing to Jesus' saving mercy, and encouraging the Christians to care for one another's needs.

(2) Acts 1–8 records some of the preaching of Peter. Acts 2:14-41 gives an account of one of Peter's sermons. When Peter presents the gospel, he emphasizes several points:

- The age of fulfillment, or the coming of the kingdom of God, is at hand. The promises of old are now fulfilled.
- This coming of the kingdom has taken place through the life, death, and resurrection of Jesus. *Jesus* is the promised one. Jesus is the Messiah.

- By virtue of this resurrection, Jesus is exalted at the right hand of God. *Jesus* is the true king. The promises are being fulfilled, Jesus is the promised Messiah, due to his resurrection.

Peter contrasts Jesus and David. David was a great man. His memory was revered. Certainly, he had made his mistakes—especially with Bathsheba. But he was ancient Israel's greatest king. When the Jews developed their idea of a coming deliverer (Messiah), they thought in terms of a successor to King David.

Jesus is this successor. However he is much greater than David. David was only a man. He was dead and buried. Jesus is more than a man. Jesus was raised from the dead. He did not stay buried. Jesus is exalted at the right hand of God. The heart of the preaching of the first Christians was the resurrected and exalted Jesus as the Messiah of God—the one who brings salvation.

(3) The Book of Acts tells of the carrying out of the promise to Abraham, that Abraham's descendants would bless all the families of the earth.

One of Peter's sermons is given in an area near the Jerusalem temple. As often Peters stresses the belief that Jesus fulfills the Old Testament. "The God of Abraham, the God of Isaac, the God of Jacob, the God of our ancestors has glorified his servant Jesus" (Acts 3:13).

He calls on his Jewish listeners to accept Jesus as their savior. "All the prophets . . . from Samuel and those after him, also predicted these days. You are the descendants of the prophets and of the covenant that God gave to your ancestors, saying to Abraham, 'And in your descendants all the families of the earth shall be blessed'" (Acts 3:24-25).

Many Jews did accept Jesus at this time, but many more did not. Yet God used those who did to spread the truth about Jesus throughout the Roman Empire—and in time the entire world.

The Book of Acts is about missionaries. It tells how the first Christians—all Jews—struggled with whether all non-Jewish people who trusted in Jesus also had to accept all the Jewish rituals and regulations.

One Christian leader, the Apostle Paul, won the debate. Non-Jewish Christians did not have to become Jews. They were a part of God's people solely because of their trust in Jesus.

Paul led the spread of the gospel. He was the greatest of the missionaries. Under Paul's leadership, Abraham's descendants indeed became a blessing to all the families of the earth.

The Book of Acts ends when Paul's missionary journey leads him to the city of Rome. Rome was the center of the Empire, the most important city in the world. The Gospel reaches even to Rome. God's blessing reaches even to Rome.

We see here how committed God is to his healing strategy. The terrible evil of the rulers of this age crucifying Jesus could not defeat that strategy. In fact the crucifixion only furthered God's healing work, because the resurrected Jesus conquered death and ended up more powerful than before.

The rulers of this age in Jerusalem continued to resist God. They violently persecuted the first Christians and drove them out of Jerusalem. However they did not defeat God. Their actions in fact actually led to a further spread of the gospel to the rest of the world.

## Questions for Thought and Discussion

1. Why did the early Christians meet with such violent persecution in Jerusalem? Why was Stephen executed? What areas of continuity of the early church with Jesus' life and teaching seem most important in this regard?

2. How do you understand the story of the early Christians speaking in tongues? Why were they doing this and what were the effects? What applications might we make from this story?

3. The Book of Acts portrays Peter in dramatically different terms than the last part of the gospel of Mark. To what would you attribute the transformation of Peter from one who denies

even knowing Jesus to one who preached openly the gospel of the risen Christ without fear of the consequences?

4. To what extent should we be expected to share our possessions as the early Christians did?

5. What do you see as the most important theological affirmations that Peter makes in his sermon in Acts 3? What might present-day preachers draw from that sermon, both in terms of content and style?

## Further Reading

On the Book of Acts: Joel B. Green, "Acts of the Apostles" in *The Dictionary of the Later New Testament and Its Developments*; Luke T. Johnson, *The Acts of the Apostles*; F. F. Bruce, *The Book of Acts*; Richard Cassidy, *Society and Politics in the Acts of the Apostles*; and Jacob Jervell, *The Theology of the Acts of the Apostles*.

# 11

# Paul, Missionary to the Gentiles—Spreading Good News to Rome (Rom. 1:1–3:31)

PAUL IS THE MOST IMPORTANT WRITER in the history of Christianity. He spells out the *meaning* of Jesus' saving work. He teaches us of God's mercy for *all* people—Jew and Gentile, male and female, slave and free.

Near the end of his life, Paul has the opportunity to write the fullest account of his understanding of the Christian faith, the letter to the Christians in Rome, what we call the book of Romans. In this letter, Paul spells out our largest dilemma as human beings—being dominated by the power of sin. He also explains God's solution to this dilemma, faith in Jesus Christ.

## The Obedience of Faith—Romans 1:1–1:17

The core of Paul's message is summarized in the phrase in Romans 1:5. Paul's goal is to help bring about "the obedience of faith." What does Paul mean by *obedience of faith*?

Paul calls on Christians to *obey* God, to *live* as God's people. Paul calls for obedience that comes from *faith*. Paul does not call for obedience that comes out of fear of what God might do to us if we are disobedient or out of anxiety about whether we are being faithful enough to make God happy with us. Paul calls for obedience that is a *response* to God's mercy. Paul calls for a response of love to love, our love responding to the love God has shown us already.

According to Paul, the obedience God wants, the obedience that comes from faith, has to do with two things—first is believing in God, trusting in God's mercy, accepting Jesus Christ as our savior from the power of sin. Second is responding to God's mercy by living mercifully ourselves, responding to God's love for us by actively loving one another and indeed the entire world.

The obedience that comes from faith is based on trust—trust in God's abundant mercy, trust that this mercy is the most important reality there is, trust that it is in being loving ourselves that we are most in harmony with God and most faithful to our purpose in life.

Paul's knowledge of God's abundant mercy and his conviction that this mercy is at the heart of reality came from his own experience of life. Paul's awareness was not just in his head, it was in his *heart*. He learned about God's mercy the hard way—through desperately needing it himself.

Paul was a Jew by birth, named Saul by his parents, after the first king of ancient Israel. By the time he was a young adult he had established himself as a leader among the Jews. He had joined with the Pharisees. He was well-educated and strongly committed to a strict understanding of religious faith.

The Pharisees believed that survival of the Jewish religion and culture in a hostile world required strictly following certain laws. Especially three laws emerged as central to this view—circumcision of males, Sabbath observance, and strict dietary restrictions. Following these laws came to be seen as the clearest way to show that the Jewish people were *different* from the outside world. This difference was the only way they could remain a distinct people. To weaken, to compromise, to disregard these differences was to threaten their very existence as a people.

Jesus experienced harsh conflicts with the Pharisees. Jesus did not always follow the food laws. He was willing to share table fellowship with unclean outsiders. Jesus did not strictly adhere to Sabbath regulations. He was willing to heal on the Sabbath. He argued that the sabbath was made for human beings, not human beings made for the sabbath. In Jesus' view, the Pharisees had made these regulations more important than human well-being.

After Jesus' death, his followers, empowered by his resurrection, continued in his ways of openness and abundant mercy. The conflicts between the Christians and the Pharisees increased, due to the Christians' continued disregard for the strict following of these laws. This conflict reached its height when one of the early church's most dynamic leaders, Stephen, was stoned.

By the time of Stephen's execution, the young Pharisee, Saul, was active. The Book of Acts tells us that when "they dragged [Stephen] out of the city and began to stone him, the witnesses laid their coats at the feet of a young man named Saul" (Acts 7:58). Saul very much supported the crowd's action.

This Saul soon became a leader among the Pharisees, specializing in persecuting Christians. He regularly breathed "threats and murder against the disciples of the Lord" (Acts 9:1). Saul was fully committed to following the ways of God as he understood them. His hostility toward the Christians was *because* of his commitment to protecting God's honor. The violence he supported and likely committed himself was because of his faith.

Later, he wrote this: "You have heard, no doubt, of my earlier life in Judaism. I was violently persecuting the church of God and was trying to destroy it. I advanced in Judaism beyond many among my people of the same age, for I was far more zealous for the traditions of my ancestors" (Gal. 1:13-14).

Then, something amazing happened. Saul headed for the city of Damascus, looking for Christians, intending to bring them back to Jerusalem to be tried for blasphemy, perhaps hoping they would all meet the same fate as Stephen.

Acts tells us what happened next. "Now as [Saul] was going along and approaching Damascus, suddenly a light from heaven flashed around him. He fell to the ground and heard a voice saying to him, 'Saul, Saul, why do you persecute me?' He asked, 'Who are you, Lord?' The reply came. 'I am Jesus, whom you are persecuting. But get up and enter the city, and you will be told what you are to do.' The men who were traveling with him stood speechless because they heard the voice but saw no one. Saul got up from the ground, and though his eyes were open, he could see nothing; so they led him by the hand and brought him into Damascus. For three days he was without sight, and neither ate nor drank" (Acts 9:3-9).

On the Damascus road and after Saul had his life turned completely around, a reality symbolized by the fact that we have come to know him by his new identity, Paul the apostle. His old world came apart. He was so undone by his experience that for three days he was in shock—he could not see, he did not eat or drink. Then he started to put the pieces together. He did so with the help of a few Christians who overcame their fear of him and began to counsel him as well as with the healing provided by God's Spirit. Even then, Paul went away, to Arabia, for three years. I imagine at least a big part of that trip was to allow himself time and space to come to terms with this new life which God had thrust upon him.

Basically what happened to Saul who became Paul was this: He was operating out of a deep, sincere desire to do God's will. He was *certain* about what that will was—to follow with rigid purity the law codes (especially circumcision, the correct diet, and Sabbath observance). Those, like the Christians, who claimed to be worshiping God but who were not following the true law codes, were *enemies*. In order faithfully to serve God, he had the responsibility to oppose, even eliminate, those impure elements. This violence was an act of service to God. Paul wanted to obey God.

Then God blew the lid off Paul's system. However, because Paul did sincerely want to do God's will, he was able to receive God's direct revelation to him. This Jesus you hate is in fact the fullest revelation of your God. This Jesus you hate is the model for genuine faithfulness to the God of Israel. It is to Paul's everlasting credit that he was able to make the switch in allegiance here.

However, it almost was too much for Paul. You can imagine. You devote your life with your whole heart to a certain path. Then, at the height of your enthusiasm, you realize you have made a tragic mistake. You realize the very acts, which you deeply believed were the best expression of faithfulness, were in fact hostile to the God you want to serve. What could be more shocking or more earthshaking?

One of the questions Paul surely struggled with long and hard is this: How could I have been so violent in the name of God? How could it have been that the more and more intensely I strove to be faithful to my religion, the more and more seriously I sinned against God?

He must also have worked at another set of questions—how can I now understand God and God's will in a way which will overcome such sacred violence? How can I strive for faithfulness in a way that will lead to righteousness and not simply more sin?

Paul speaks out of his own experience when he writes Romans. As an alternative to doing violence in the name of obedience to God, he writes of obedience that comes from faith. The obedience that comes from faith is what the "gospel of God" produces.

The gospel of God is the good news that, more than anything else, God loves us and wants us to be whole. In *response* to God's love, we are challenged ourselves to love. This is the most important law or commandment. Paul makes this clear later in Romans. "The one who loves another has fulfilled the law. The commandments, 'You shall not commit adultery; You shall not murder; You shall not steal; You shall not covet'; and any other commandment, are summed up in this word. 'Love your neighbor as yourself'" (Rom. 13:8-9).

Paul's story, then, has the issues of healing and shalom right at the center. In the name of God, Saul committed violence. Most violence is like Saul's—taking life for the sake of a perceived greater good, often directly as a service to one's God.

Saul's conversion was, in effect, a conversion to understanding that God never wants violence—the greatest commandment is to *love*. This commandment trumps everything else.

In his desire to do good, the violent, pre-conversion Paul (Saul) in reality did bad things. In his desire to be faithful to his religion, Paul drove a wedge between himself and God. In his desire to be morally upright, Paul sinned.

Years later, after finding out what genuine faithfulness is— trusting in Jesus Christ as the true Son of God, after learning more and more what it means to live in the light of God's mercy, Paul writes Romans as an answer to the way he used to think. The person Paul is arguing against in Romans is actually himself from those old days.

## Sin and Its Solution—Romans 1:18–3:31

In the first chapter of Romans, in his words against the "ungodliness and wickedness" of the world, Paul sets the stage for his deeper concerns. His critique of the outside world is only a preliminary. His *bigger* concern is to make a point aimed at the faith community—at "good" people who do bad things.

Paul challenges his readers' smugness about their own righteousness and security as God's people. See how bad those worldly people are, he starts out. Yeah, yeah, his readers, "good" people that they are, would have replied. Those bad people worship idols. They deserve God's wrath.

But then comes a shock. Chapter 2 begins with some harsh words aimed precisely at those who are so quick to point fingers.

"You have no excuse, whoever you are, when you judge others; for in passing judgment on another you condemn yourself, because you, the judge, are doing the very same things" (Rom. 2:1).

Paul has set up his readers here in a way which parallels how Nathan set up David with the story of the sheep-owner victimized by the rich man, and, especially, how Amos sets up his listeners by prophesying against the evil outside nations.

Paul starts with the discussions of worldly sins in Romans one to drive home his point in 2:1—"you do the same things." Good people can be sinners too—committing violence in the name of purity, survival of a peoplehood, faithfulness to God.

Of the sins Paul lists at the end of chapter 1, several are ones "good" people are particularly vulnerable to (including the old Paul): covetousness, haughtiness, heartlessness all come to mind.

(1) "Being filled with . . . covetousness"—comparing oneself to others, desiring to be the most impressive, wanting acclaim. This is the kind of sin James and John committed when they asked Jesus if they could sit at his right hand in glory. They wanted everyone to know what great disciples they had been. They wanted everyone to see what faithful people they were.

Paul is saying, When I point fingers at those I condemn as terrible sinners I may be blinded to my own covetousness. In my zealousness to stamp out others' sins, I run a great risk of being stamped out by my own sin. My attitude toward others needs to be compassion and mercy—just as God's is toward me in my sin. If I am blinded to my sin in my pride, I will not realize how merciful God truly is. And I will miss the boat.

(2) "Haughty"—scornful of others, disdainful, superior. What Paul especially has in mind in naming this sin is the pride he used to have about being a Jew. He was born into a special people. His people knew God, knew the truth, knew the ways of righteousness better than others did. If I am so certain of my own superiority over others, why would I need God's mercy? And how honest will I be able to be about my own sinfulness?

(3) A third sin Paul mentions is "heartless." Like covetousness and haughtiness, heartlessness is a sin "good" people are prone to. Paul himself showed terrible heartlessness when he participated in the stoning of Stephen, the great early Christian leader. "Heartless" is synonymous with lacking compassion, with being harsh and insensitive. Heartlessness is always a danger when one is zealous for purity, for the "truth," for obedience to commandments and laws. Heartlessness is always a danger when love is secondary to some other value.

The most hurtful result of these sins of the "morally upright" is that they keep the community of faith from serving as a light to the nations. What we have to offer the world is an awareness of God's mercy, God's healing compassion. The community of faith is meant to serve as an agent of God's healing strategy for our broken world.

Paul, in Romans 1–3, moves toward his conclusion that all people are sinful—good people *and* bad people alike, blatant sinners and morally upright sinners. All people are in need of God's mercy. And the final part of Paul's argument is that God's mercy is available, to everyone, without distinction. God's mercy is available to Jew and Gentile. God's mercy is available to the morally upright sinner and to the blatant sinner. In fact, God does not even make these kinds of distinctions. To God we are *all* loved people, all worthwhile people, all people who matter, all people who can, and who must, accept God's mercy. And we are all people who can, and who must, share this mercy with others.

Paul's punch line comes in 3:21. "But now, apart from the law, the righteousness of God has been disclosed . . . [to justify,] by God's grace as a gift [all who trust in that grace, which God has made known through Jesus]." Paul's punch line is that the answer to sin is trusting in God's mercy.

The key term in 3:21 is "righteousness of God." The Greek word for righteousness is *dikaiosune*. It is the word that translates the Hebrew words *mishpat* and *sedeqeh*—"justice" and "righteousness." They are roughly synonymous and suggest "restoration," "wholeness," "setting things right," "healing that which was broken."

Paul is saying that the justice of God ("healing that which was broken") is not primarily expressed by doing works of the law—strict boundary lines between us and them, means of showing (through circumcision, kosher, Sabbath) that we are righteous. It is expressed by trusting in God's mercy shown through Jesus Christ.

It follows that the fruit of this trust, the lived-out expression of being justified, is reconciliation among human beings. The Letter to the Ephesians spells this out explicitly. The wall dividing Jew and Gentile is abolished for those who trust in Christ.

Justice has to do with reconciliation. This point takes on much more weight when we think of Paul's own story—moving from violence toward peace as a result of meeting Jesus.

## Questions for Thought and Discussion

1. Paul writes Romans to foster what he calls "the obedience of faith." These terms *obedience* and *faith* are often seen to be in tension with each other. Why would Paul use them together? What does he mean? How would you apply his teaching about "the obedience of faith" to your life?

2. Do you agree that understanding Paul's personal experience of meeting Jesus is crucial for understanding his theology? What do you see as the connection?

3. Can you think of parallels to Paul's experience of religious legalism fostering violence? Is this an inherent temptation with organized religion?

4. Do you agree that there is actually continuity concerning the meaning of the law as it was originally intended, Jesus' teaching about the law, and Paul's views of the law? What is the positive value of the law in a mercy-oriented approach to faith?

5. Are you vulnerable to Paul's critique of judgmentalism in Romans 2? How do you think the appropriate balance might be struck between avoiding judgmentalism yet still living according to strong moral convictions?

6. Can you think of examples today where "sins of the morally upright" within the community of faith hinder our calling to be "a blessing for all the families of the earth"?

7. How do you understand Paul's teaching on "justification by faith" and the ramifications of that teaching for Christian living?

## Further Reading

The writings of Paul are some of the most diversely interpreted of all the materials in the Bible. My thinking has been especially shaped by the work of James D. G. Dunn. His programmatic essay, "A New Perspective on Paul," first presented in 1982 and now published in *Jesus, Paul, and the Law*, summarizes the main issues and gives Dunn's perspective. Dunn's mature (and quite detailed!) position is presented in *The Theology of Paul the Apostle*. Robert G. Hamerton-Kelly, *Sacred Violence: Paul's Hermeneutic of the Cross*, has helped me think about issues of violence in relation to Paul's theology.

Other important books on Paul which I have found helpful include: Neil Elliott, *Liberating Paul: The Justice of God and the Politics of the Apostle*; N. T. Wright, *The Climax of the Covenant: Christ and Law in Pauline Theology*; Ralph Martin, *Reconciliation: A Study of Paul's Theology*; Jerome Murphy-O'Connor, *Paul: A Critical Life*; Daniel Boyarin, *A Radical Jew: Paul and the Politics of Identity*; Victor Paul Furnish, *The Moral Teaching of Paul: Selected Issues*; Krister Stendahl, *Paul Among Jews and Gentiles*; and Alan Segal, *Paul the Convert: The Apostolate and Apostasy of Saul the Pharisee*.

On Romans, Dunn's extensive two-volume commentary, *Romans*, provides detailed and impressive exegetical and theological insights. Other useful studies: David Hay and Elizabeth Johnson, eds., *Pauline Theology: Romans*; Peter Stuhlmacher, *Paul's Letter to the Romans: A Commentary*; David Kaylor, *Paul's Covenant Community: Jew and Gentile in Romans*; and John Ziesler, *Paul's Letter to the Romans.*

# 12

# The Book of Revelation—
# Christianity Under Fire

*T*HE EARLY CHRISTIANS CONTINUED TO FACE persecution throughout the first century of Christianity—and beyond. Some persecution by Jewish religious leaders continued, due to their denial
that Jesus was the promised Messiah. That is, this conflict was
over who genuinely represented God's healing strategy.

As time went on, though, a much greater and more deadly
source of persecution emerged—the Roman Empire. One of the
great spectator sports became sending the Christians to the lions.
People known to be Christians were sent into arenas with hungry
lions. The sport was to see how long they would survive.

The problem with the Roman Empire was *religious*. Basically it came down to whom the people would worship—the
God of Jesus Christ or the emperor-as-god.

At about the same time as Christianity emerged, the practice
in the Empire of worshiping the emperor as divine also emerged.
One main reason for this was that the Roman Empire included a
huge area, with many different nationalities. A common religion
of emperor worship was a way to unify these different peoples.

Faithful Christians, of course, could not worship the emperor. That would have been blatant idolatry for them. By refusing such worship, they threatened the social unity based on common religious practices. The Christians paid a price for this refusal—threats, persecution, even death.

The stress of living in this context of constant danger challenged the faith of many Christians. The final book of the Bible,
the Book of Revelation, was written to encourage Christians in
the face of these dangers. It was written to let them know that
God would remain faithful to them come what may.

Revelation is a notoriously difficult book to interpret. It contains many weird images, cryptic numbers, cosmic upheaval,
violence, judgment, and a great deal of symbolism. Is it about the
future—or is it actually about the first century A.D.?

I recognize that Christians hold widely divergent understandings of Revelation. I am among those who believe Revelation was written to address the needs of people in the first century (not primarily to give a blueprint of the future). The author
of Revelation, a Christian prophet named John, wrote this book
to provide encouragement to Christians in Asia Minor (the western part of present-day Turkey).

These Christians faced a double-pronged set of challenges;
either face persecution for their faithfulness to the way of Jesus or
be tempted to conform to their wider culture. Such conformity
might protect them from persecution, but according to John it
threatens to separate them from God.

So, in a highly imaginative and symbolic set of visions, John
challenges the hearts of his readers. Remain faithful to the way of
Jesus. Turn from the allurements of Roman civilization because
this civilization is based not on trust in God but on trust in the
powers of evil (symbolized in Revelation by characters such as
the Beast, the Dragon, and the Great Whore).

If Revelation is prophecy (as the book itself claims to be), it
is prophecy in the same sense that, say, the Book of Amos is
prophecy. That is, prophecy that "forth-tells" the will of God in
a challenging situation where the conventional wisdom of the
day (and all too many people in the faith community) supports
ways of life based on a rejection of God's will. To the extent that
such prophecy foretells the future, it does so in service of chal-

lenging its readers to turn back to God's ways in the present. The foretelling of Revelation is for the sake of the ethics of its original readers, not to provide detailed information about a far-off future.

However, Revelation does offer words of hope and encouragement for Christians of all ages—especially those facing persecution and temptations from their culture to worship things other than the God of Jesus Christ. Revelation speaks to us insofar as we share the general characteristics of its first readers: needing to be confronted for too easily conforming to our culture or needing to be encouraged to remain faithful to Jesus' way even in the face of suffering and persecution.

Revelation is full of symbolism, from start to finish, and it takes some interpreting to figure out what this symbolism is about. Here I share a modest number of my interpretations.

There are three passages I want briefly to mention (Rev. 5, 13–14, 21–22). Each passage speaks to the need for fearful Christians to find assurance that their God remains the true God—and that they can and must continue to trust in God and worship God alone.

### Revelation 5:1-14—The Triumph of the Lamb

One of the common motifs in Revelation is that of conquering, or overcoming. In face of the seemingly all-conquering power of the Roman Empire to deal out death, Christians are told of another type of conquering. This type of conquering is not about killing others but about remaining faithful to Jesus, faithful to God. It is about remaining faithful even to the point of suffering, even to the point of death itself.

How is this "conquering"? It can be seen as conquering *only* if one believes this is precisely how Jesus won his victory—remaining faithful, not resorting to violence, facing death itself—and being vindicated by God. Revelation 5 draws on this core conviction of Christian faith to encourage its readers. Jesus

Christ is the true victor, the true conqueror. Jesus won his way to eternal life through his faithfulness even to death.

Revelation 5 presents the most crucial image of the book. The chapter begins with a scroll. Exactly what this scroll is we cannot say for sure. It seems to have some large meaning. It needs to be opened for the meaning and direction of history to be known, maybe even for God's purposes to be fulfilled.

At first we are told, though, that no one can be found to open the scroll. Is history at an impasse? The writer says he weeps. But then—"Do not weep, one has been found." Who has the kind of power needed to open the great scroll? We are told it is the Lion of the Tribe of Judah. Here is the crucial moment. The victor, the conqueror, is "a Lamb standing as if it had been slain" (Rev. 5:6). This Lamb is none other than Jesus Christ, slain but now standing, risen from the dead.

Jesus is the conqueror. This image is meant to encourage his followers. The power that truly matters is not the power to kill (the kind of power Rome wields). Rather, true power is the power to trust in God and thus to face even death faithfully. This trust is worth giving because the Lamb that was slain now stands. The power Jesus expressed is the strongest power in the cosmos. It is the power of love, which is everlasting.

This first vision communicates the core affirmation of Revelation. Jesus alone (and not the emperor) is Lord and to be worshiped. He is the truth—and genuinely powerful.

## Revelation 13:1–14:5—Dealing with the Beast

In chapter 13, we are introduced to the terrible Beast. We are shown a Beast whose power is not that of wealth, but that of government (with its "crowns" and "throne"). His authority is worldwide. This symbolizes the Roman Empire—or perhaps you could say the spiritual power behind the Roman Empire.

Rome demanded that people worship the emperor. This was a terrible blasphemy for Christians—blatant idolatry. This was

Satanic, pure evil. Revelation 13:4 speaks of this: "The whole earth . . . worshiped the dragon [meaning Satan], for he had given his authority to the Beast [meaning the Empire], and they worshiped the Beast, saying 'Who is like the Beast, and who can fight against it?'" Emperor worship is simply worshiping Satan.

Christians are challenged not to go along with this worship—and to expect to pay a cost for their refusal. But they are not to fight back with violence. Revelation 13:10 tells them: "If you are to be taken captive, into captivity you go; if you kill with the sword, with the sword you must be killed. Here is a call for the endurance and faith of the saints."

Just as Jesus stuck to the path of non-retaliation even in the face of violence, so too must his followers. Fighting the Beast's violence with violence only leads to more violence. What calls for patient endurance is Christians submitting without violent resistance to the conquering attack of the Beast, since only in this way can the spiral of violence be broken. To repay violence with violence only perpetuates violence.

The first few verses in chapter 14 stand in important contrast to chapter 13. Revelation 13 shows the true nature of Roman emperor worship. Christians need to say no even if it means suffering and tribulation. The purpose, then, of 14:1-5 is to show the deeper reality; the Lamb is victorious and that those who follow him are also victorious. That conquering the Beast was only temporary. The faithful one's final fate is to sing on God's mountain, Mt. Zion.

The central message of Revelation is that the Lamb of God has defeated the powers of evil. It will take time for the full effects of this victory to be manifested. There may be some hard times before the victory takes full effect—but it will. In the meantime, even as they face suffering and persecution, Christians can also praise God.

The relevance of the vision of the multitude singing in Revelation 14 is to encourage Christians. The way to resist the Beast is, as 14:4 says, to "follow the Lamb wherever he goes." Chapter 5 tells us that the Lamb who was slain is the master of history. The Lamb who defeated evil through the way of love is the model.

This second set of visions, of the Beast and of the faithful ones singing praise to God, shows two aspects of the reality of Revelation's readers. It reveals, first, that the persecuting Roman Empire is aligned with Satan and must not be worshiped. Second, it shows that as Jesus' followers are faithful in following the Lamb, they will be present with God.

## Revelation 21:1–22:7—
## God's Completed Healing Strategy

The concluding vision in Revelation, of the New Jerusalem, reveals God's completed healing strategy. This was the enlivening hope that would help Christians remain strong and faithful, even when things got difficult.

"See, the home of God is among mortals. God will dwell with them as their God; they will be God's people, and God will be with them; God will wipe every tear from their eyes. Death will be no more; mourning and crying and pain will be no more." The New Jerusalem is a place cleansed of the forces of evil, creation as it was intended to be. Healing is completed.

The New Jerusalem is pictured as being made up of *people*. "On the gates are inscribed the names of the twelve tribes of Israel" (Rev. 21:12) and "on the foundations are inscribed the twelve names of the twelve apostles of the Lamb" (Rev. 21:14). This symbolizes the entire people of God. The earthly temple is no more because these people now live in the direct presence of God.

God's glory fills everything. Merely to be in the city is to be with God. An important part of this vision of fulfilled hopes, along with the end of evil and the direct presence of God, is the promise of the *healing* of the nations. The human enemies of

God's people are not, in the final event, to be destroyed. They, too, will find healing—not necessarily all of them, but those who turn to the true God when the dragon's, or deceiver's, spell is broken. Part of the reason Jesus' followers do not fight back and join the spiral of violence is this hope that even the nations may find healing. Persevering love is the method—not brute force.

The New Jerusalem, Revelation 22:1-2 tells us, contains a river, with the water of life. On each side of the river is the tree of life. "The leaves of this tree are for the healing of the nations." Revelation 21 and 22 affirms that this fulfillment, this conclusion of history, will be worth all the pain and struggle humankind has experienced throughout the ages.

Most of Revelation portrays the spiritual forces of evil, symbolized by the dragon and his cohorts, as powerful and greatly influencing life on earth. They are behind the persecutions, injustice, and sufferings that plague people of faith. The conclusion, though, in Revelation 21 and 22, is that this evil will not last forever. God is not powerless to stop it. The power of everlasting love will win out. God's healing strategy will conclude with its mission accomplished.

This final vision, the vision of the New Jerusalem, offers encouragement to the persecuted Christians to persevere. Christians are challenged to trust that despite how difficult things might be in the present, God's purposes will be fulfilled.

## Questions for Thought and Discussion

1. Why do you think the Roman Empire persecuted Christians? Are there parallels with persecution of Christians today? Can you imagine being persecuted for your faith? Under what circumstances?

2. What kind of impression did you have of the Book of Revelation before reading this chapter? What do you think of the perspective proposed here? Are you comfortable with the suggestion that Revelation needs to be understood more in terms of

how it spoke to the first-century world and less in terms of its predictions about the future?

3. What difference do you think it makes to make central to one's interpretation the point that this book is a "revelation of *Jesus Christ*"?

4. How do you understand the Lamb to "conquer" (Rev. 5)? What is conquered? Why? How? What relevance to our lives are the answers we give to these questions? That is, what difference does it make in our lives for us to think of the Lamb's conquering in the way we do?

5. In what way did the Roman Empire demand people's allegiance? Why would John and other Christians have seen this as idolatrous? Are there parallels in our world today?

6. How do you respond to the claims of Revelation that God has *already* defeated the powers of evil? How do you think of these claims in relation to the world as you see it around you? In what way (if any) does it make sense in light of our world to say that the powers of evil are defeated?

7. Is the vision of the New Jerusalem a source of hope for you? Why or why not? How literally do you expect it to be fulfilled? How will we get there?

## Further Reading

Contrary to the general impression many people have—that Revelation is all about future predictions—a surprising number of studies of Revelation take a more symbolic, ethically aware perspective. I have applied the interpretative framework used above to the entire book of Revelation in *Triumph of the Lamb.*

Studies which I have found to be particularly helpful include Allan Boesak, *Comfort and Protest: The Apocalypse from a South African Perspective*; Eugene Boring, *Revelation*; Richard Bauckham, *The Theology of the Book of Revelation*; George Caird, *The Revelation of St. John the Divine*; Jacques Ellul, *Apocalypse: The Book of Revelation*; Ward Ewing, *The Power of the Lamb*;

Wilfrid Harrington, *Revelation*; Gerhard Krodel, *Revelation*; J.P.M. Sweet, *Revelation*; Arthur Wainwright, *Mysterious Apocalypse: Interpreting the Book of Revelation* (a fascinating history of how Revelation has been interpreted); and Robert Wall, *Revelation*.

# 13

# Reflections on God's Healing Strategy

*I*N THE INTRODUCTION TO THIS VOLUME, I proposed that the Bible is best read as the story of God's healing strategy—which is to say, as the story of God's reconciling mercy and love as it intersects with human history. Acknowledging that we could only scratch the surface in this short book, I proposed as we take the various threads of biblical faith together, we see a portrayal of God as persevering in love, patient in forgiveness, ceaselessly initiating restoration in the divine/human relationship.

I have only been able to illustrate this proposal in these pages, but we have seen continuity from the original portrayal of human beings in the Garden of Eden to the concluding vision of uncountable numbers of people in the New Jerusalem. As the hymn "Amazing Grace" states, between these two pictures we may trace "many dangers, toils, and snares."

The initial picture of human life in the early verses of Genesis shows us God's good creation, human beings being made in God's own image and given responsibilities for growth and cultivation in the wider world. God and human beings are relational, connected to one another through love freely offered and freely received.

Early on, a shadow falls as the freedom and relationality of the first human beings turn to their disadvantage; they reject their limits before God. As Adam and Eve disregard their finitude, seeking God-like knowledge, they trigger a dynamic of brokenness, fear, anxiety, and self-regard. Creation itself is shaken. Right away, human relationality becomes a curse as Cain slays his own brother out of jealousy and frustration.

Nonetheless, even in the face of the eruption of disharmony and alienation, God remains committed to these beings God has made. Adam and Eve, and later Cain, reap serious consequences for their acts, but God gives them time and space. God's persevering love means the connecting link between God and human beings, while greatly shaken and wounded, is not altogether severed. Possibilities for restoration remain.

The story of the great flood during the time of Noah seems at first glance to indicate that God's patience came to an end. But the final message of the story underscores God's ongoing commitment. The story can be read as a dramatization of God's ambivalence in the face of the disharmony and self-destructive autonomy human existence manifests. But the story concludes with God's clear and unequivocal commitment to the relationship. God promises to confront human brokenness not with brutal chaos, but with gentle, everlasting, healing love.

After the waters recede, the next major step God takes is a new act of creation. God calls Abraham and Sarah to be the founders of a community of people who will know God, and with the knowledge to serve as a "blessing for all the families of the earth." With this act, God's healing strategy begins: a people who know God's mercy start to become a conduit of mercy for others, ultimately bringing healing for all nations. According to various New Testament writings, this promise to Abraham and Sarah of their descendants being agents of healing for the world remains in effect. Jesus himself is understood as God's fulfillment of this promise (see, for example, Luke 1:55; Acts 3:13; Romans 4:1-25).

The legacy, as we all know, of the success of Abraham's descendants in blessing the peoples of the earth is mixed. The Old

Testament stories we have considered in this book make that clear. We could say the same about the stories of the Christian church in the past 2,000 years. Often the calling of the community of faith has been understood more as an invitation to self-exaltation and self-aggrandizement than as a calling to service and unconditional mercy.

Nonetheless, the biblical story as well as many stories in the centuries since the final biblical writings point toward a healing reality in the lives of people of faith. The fact that I, a descendant in part of fierce Nordic warriors, now write as a convinced follower of Jesus reflects the spread of the good news to "all the ends of the earth" (Acts 1:8).

Christians (and Jews) confess that this promise to Abraham perseveres. We point back to ways God has acted on the promise as evidence. We also point forward to a vision of completed healing. In both cases, looking back and looking forward, we find encouragement for the task of seeking to live in light of the promise in our present.

Psalm 77 tells of one process of the writer finding himself in deep discouragement—"I am so troubled that I cannot speak" (Ps. 77:4). In his grief, he "calls to mind the deeds of the Lord" (Ps. 77:11), and muses on God's mighty acts. In particular, the writer calls to mind the liberation of the Israelite slaves from Egypt. In so doing, the writer makes present a sense that God remains a liberating God. God remains a God who cares for people in pain, a God who offers on-going healing. The memory of God's past involvement reduces the despair of the perceived abandonment in the present. This memory, in fact, offers a basis for hope that the present will change as well.

A second element, along with remembrance of past healing experiences, is a bold hope for future healing. Isaiah prophesies the establishment of the Lord's house on the highest of the mountains. People from many nations will flock to it to learn the ways of God. "They shall beat their swords into plowshares, and their spears into pruning hooks; nation shall not lift up sword against nation, neither shall they learn war any more" (Isa. 2:4).

Revelation 22 repeats a similar hope. "The angel showed me the river of the water of life, bright as crystal, flowing from the throne of God and of the Lamb through the middle of the street of the city. On either side of the river is the tree of life with its twelve kinds of fruit, producing its fruit each month; and the leaves of the tree are for the healing of the nations" (Rev. 22:1-2).

The point of both the remembering and the looking ahead is that these awarenesses tell us about God. God is a God allied with slaves. God is a God who hears the cries of the oppressed. God is a God allied with the transformation of swords into plowshares. God is a God concerned with *healing* the nations.

In our world of brokenness and alienation, of cynicism and despair, we need such a message of hope for healing more than ever. The biblical message of God's healing strategy, however, encourages us not only to remember God's past deeds of healing and transformation but also to gain courage from such memories. The Bible invites us as well to draw on its visions to find hope for the future.

The biblical message of God's healing strategy also gives us concrete guidance for our present lives. This message directs us to communities of faith, communities that resist the power politics of our day by their practices of mutual respect, of collaborative decision-making, of practical support for people in need. This message directs us to trust in God's mercy, the good news that Jesus indeed is still among us, sharing bread with sinners and outcasts, forgiving enemies, calling into question institutional violence.

This message offers us a healing perspective on life directly relevant to our present world. God's healing strategy challenges us to share in mutual relationships in the face of a culture that pushes us to autonomy and isolation. We are challenged to see life as trustworthy, the locus of God's abundant love, amid a culture which understands life to be a dog-eat-dog, competitive proposition in a world in which the most important resources are to be hoarded and competed for. We are challenged to order our common life in terms of equal regard, not hierarchies in which the strong dominate the weak, the privileged exploit the less advantaged.

God's persevering love, even in the face of countless seeming defeats, speaks of a different kind of power as fundamental in the universe. God's healing power is power that does not coerce, that does not domineer. God's power empowers others. God is powerful enough to let people say no, to allow people to choose to reciprocate.

God's justice restores relationships and mends what is broken. God's justice brings healing, not vengeance and retribution. God's healing strategy does not require punishment and separation, just as it does not coerce conformity.

When Jesus called his followers to "be merciful, as God is merciful" (Luke 6:36), he summarized God's way of bringing healing to the world. And he highlighted the central way that we may be part of God's healing work.

## Questions for Thought and Discussion

1. Reflect on your understanding of the message(s) of the Bible. How do you respond to the argument of this book concerning the theme of "God's healing strategy"? Do you find this a helpful way of summarizing the Bible's core message?

2. What do you believe to be the Bible's central relevance for Christian living in our world today? How would you apply themes we have looked at in this book?

3. Recognizing that this book has been highly selective in its treatment of the Bible, do you think other biblical materials would, by and large, support the argument of this book? Think of examples that offer support and examples which stand in tension.

4. If you are not comfortable with "God's healing strategy" as a summary of the Bible's core message, do you have an alternative to suggest? What materials would you offer in support of your statement? Or do you believe that the Bible is simply too diverse to fit within one general theme? If this is the case, what are the implications for how we read and apply the Bible?

5. If you were going to pick one passage from the Bible as a key window for viewing what the Bible has to offer our world, what would it be?

# Bibliography

Alter, Robert and Frank Kermode, eds. *The Literary Guide to the Bible*. Cambridge, Mass.: Harvard University Press, 1987.

Alter, Robert. *Genesis: Translation and Commentary*. New York: Norton, 1996.

Alter, Robert. *The Art of Biblical Narrative*. New York: Basic Books, 1981.

Anderson, Bernhard W. *From Creation to New Creation: Old Testament Perspectives*. Minneapolis: Fortress Press, 1994.

Bailie, Gil. *Violence Unveiled: Humanity at the Crossroads*. New York: Crossroad Publishing Co., 1995.

Bauckham, Richard. *The Theology of the Book of Revelation*. New York: Cambridge University Press, 1993.

Beeby, H. D. *Grace Abounding: Hosea*. International Theological Commentary. Grand Rapids, Mich.: Eerdmans, 1989.

Berrigan, Daniel. *Minor Prophets, Major Themes*. Marion, SD: Fortkamp Publishing, 1995.

Birch, Bruce C. "1 and 2 Samuel." In *New Interpreters Bible*, vol. 2. Leander Keck, ed. Nashville: Abingdon Press, 1998. pp. 947-1383.

Birch, Bruce C. *Let Justice Roll Down: The Old Testament, Ethics, and Christian Life*. Louisville: Westminster/John Knox Press, 1991.

Birch, Bruce C. *What Does the Lord Require? The Old Testament Call to Social Witness.* Philadelphia: Westminster Press, 1985.

Boesak, Allan A. *Comfort and Protest: The Apocalypse from a South African Perspective.* Philadelphia: Westminster Press, 1987.

Borg, Marcus J. *Jesus, A New Vision: Spirit, Culture, and the Life of Discipleship.* San Francisco: Harper and Row, 1987.

Boring, M. Eugene. *Revelation.* Interpretation Commentary. Louisville: John Knox Press, 1989.

Boyarin, Daniel. *A Radical Jew: Paul and the Politics of Identity.* Berkeley, Calif.: University of California Press, 1994.

Breech, James. *The Silence of Jesus: The Authentic Voice of the Historical Man.* Philadelphia: Fortress Press, 1983.

Bruce, F. F. *The Book of Acts.* New International Commentary. Grand Rapids, Mich.: Eerdmans, 1988.

Brueggemann, Walter. "Exodus." In *The New Interpreters Bible*, vol. 1. Leander Keck, ed. Nashville: Abingdon Press, 1994. pp. 675-981.

——. *A Social Reading of the Old Testament: Prophetic Approaches to Israel's Communal Life.* Minneapolis: Fortress Press, 1994.

——. *David's Truth in Israel's Imagination and Memory.* Minneapolis: Fortress Press, 1985.

——. *Genesis.* Interpretation Commentary. Atlanta: John Knox Press, 1982.

——. *Interpretation and Obedience: From Faithful Reading to Faithful Living.* Minneapolis: Fortress Press, 1991.

——. *Living Toward a Vision: Biblical Reflections on Shalom.* United Church Press, 1976.

——. *Old Testament Theology: Essays on Structure, Theme, and Text.* Minneapolis: Fortress Press, 1992.

————. *The Bible Makes Sense*. Winona, Minn.: St. Mary's Press, 1977.

————. *The Land: Place and Gift, Promise, and Challenge in Biblical Faith*. Philadelphia: Fortress Press, 1977.

————. *Theology of the Old Testament: Testimony, Dispute, Advocacy*. Minneapolis: Fortress Press, 1997.

————. *The Prophetic Imagination*. Philadelphia: Fortress Press, 1978.

————. *Tradition for Crisis: Hosea*. Atlanta: John Knox Press, 1968.

————. *1 Kings*. Knox Preaching Guides. Louisville: John Knox Press, 1982.

————. *2 Kings*. Knox Preaching Guides. Louisville: John Knox Press, 1982.

Cahill, Thomas. *The Gifts of the Jews: How a Tribe of Desert Nomads Changed the Way Everyone Thinks and Feels*. New York: Doubleday, 1998.

Caird, George B. *The Revelation of St. John the Divine*. Harper's New Testament Commentaries. New York: Harper and Row, 1966.

Cassidy, Richard J. *Society and Politics in the Acts of the Apostles*. Maryknoll, N.Y: Orbis Books, 1987.

Childs, Brevard S. *Old Testament Theology in a Canonical Context*. Philadelphia: Fortress Press, 1985.

Coote, Robert C. *Amos Among the Prophets: Composition and Theology*. Philadelphia: Fortress Press, 1981.

Crosby, Michael H. *Spirituality of the Beatitudes: Matthew's Challenge for First World Christians*. Maryknoll, N.Y.: Orbis Books, 1981.

Davenport, Gene L. *Into the Darkness: Discipleship in the Sermon on the Mount*. Nashville: Abingdon Press, 1988.

Donahue, John. *The Gospel in Parable*. Philadelphia: Fortress Press, 1988.

Douglass, James W. *The Nonviolent Coming of God.* Maryknoll, N.Y.: Orbis Books, 1991.

Dunn, James D. G. *Jesus, Paul, and the Law: Studies in Mark and Galatians.* Louisville: Westminster/John Knox Press, 1990.

———. *Romans.* Word Biblical Commentary. Dallas: Word Books, 1988.

———. *The Theology of Paul the Apostle.* Grand Rapids, Mich: Eerdmans, 1997.

Edwards, George R. *Jesus and the Politics of Violence.* New York: Harper and Row, 1972.

Elliott, Neil. *Liberating Paul: The Justice of God and the Politics of the Apostle.* Maryknoll, N.Y.: Orbis Books, 1994.

Ellul, Jacques. *Apocalypse: The Book of Revelation.* New York: Seabury Press, 1977.

———. *The Meaning of the City.* Grand Rapids, Mich.: Eerdmans, 1970.

———. *The Politics of God and the Politics of Man.* Grand Rapids, Mich.: Eerdmans, 1972.

Ewing, Ward. *The Power of the Lamb: Revelation's Theology of Liberation for You.* Cambridge, Mass.: Cowley Publications, 1990.

Fretheim, Terence E. "Genesis." In *New Interpreters Bible*, vol. 1. Leander Keck, ed. Nashville: Abingdon Press, 1994. pp. 319-674.

———. *Exodus.* Interpretation Commentary. Louisville: John Knox Press, 1991.

———. *The Suffering of God: An Old Testament Perspective.* Philadelphia: Fortress Press, 1984.

Frye, Northrup. *The Great Code: The Bible and Literature.* New York: Harcourt, Brace, and Jovanovich, 1982.

Furnish, Victor Paul. *The Moral Teaching of Paul: Selected Issues.* Nashville: Abingdon Press, 1979.

Gill, Athol. *Life on the Road: The Gospel Basis for a Messianic Lifestyle.* Scottdale, Pa.: Herald Press, 1989.

Goergen, Donald J. *The Mission and Ministry of Jesus.* Wilmington, Del.: Michael Glazier, 1986.

———. *The Death and Resurrection of Jesus.* Wilmington, Del.: Michael Glazier, 1988. •

Gottwald, Norman K. *The Tribes of Yahweh: A Sociology of the Religion of Liberated Israel, 1250-1050 BCE.* Maryknoll, N.Y.: Orbis Books, 1979.

Gowan, Donald E. "Amos." In *New Interpreters Bible*, vol. 7. Leander Keck, ed. Nashville: Abingdon Press, 1996. pp. 337-432.

Green, Joel B. "Acts of the Apostles." In *The Dictionary of the Later New Testament and Its Developments.* Ralph P. Martin and Peter H. Davids, eds. Downers Grove, Ill.: InterVarsity Press, 1997. pp. 7-24.

Grimsrud, Ted. *Triumph of the Lamb: A Self-Study Guide to the Book of Revelation.* Scottdale, Pa.: Herald Press, 1987.

Hamerton-Kelly, Robert G. *Sacred Violence: Paul's Hermeneutic of the Cross.* Minneapolis: Fortress Press, 1992.

Hanson, Paul D. *Isaiah 40–66.* Interpretation Commentary. Louisville: John Knox Press, 1995.

———. *The People Called: The Growth of Community in the Bible.* New York: Harper and Row, 1986.

Harrelson, Walter. *The Ten Commandments and Human Rights.* Philadelphia: Fortress Press, 1980.

Harrington, Wilfrid J. *Revelation.* Sacra Pagina. Collegeville, Minn.: Michael Glazier, 1993.

Hay, David M. and E. Elizabeth Johnson, eds. *Pauline Theology: Volume 3: Romans.* Minneapolis: Fortress Press, 1995.

Hays, Richard B. *The Moral Vision of the New Testament: A Contemporary Introduction to New Testament Ethics.* San Francisco: HarperCollins, 1996.

Heschel, Abraham J. *The Prophets*. New York: Harper and Row, 1962.

Holladay, William L. *Long Ago God Spoke: How Christians May Hear the Old Testament Today*. Minneapolis: Fortress Press, 1995.

Hooker, Morna. *The Gospel According to Saint Mark*. Black's New Testament Commentary. Peabody, MA: Hendrickson Publishers, 1991.

Janzen, Waldemar. *Old Testament Ethics: A Paradigmatic Approach*. Louisville: Westminster/John Knox Press, 1994.

Jervell, Jacob. *The Theology of the Acts of the Apostles*. New York: Cambridge University Press, 1996.

Johnson, Luke T. *The Acts of the Apostles*. Sacra Pagina. Collegeville, Minn.: Michael Glazier, 1992.

———. *Sharing Possessions: Mandate and Symbol of Faith*. Philadelphia: Fortress Press, 1981.

Jones, G. H. *1 and 2 Kings*. The New Century Bible Commentary. Grand Rapids, Mich.: Eerdmans, 1984.

Josipovici, Gabriel. *The Book of God: A Response to the Bible*. New Haven, Conn.: Yale University Press, 1988.

Kaylor, R. David. *Paul's Covenant Community: Jew and Gentile in Romans*. Atlanta: John Knox Press, 1988.

Kelber, Werner H. *Mark's Story of Jesus*. Philadelphia: Fortress Press, 1979.

Klein, Ralph W. *Israel in Exile: A Theological Interpretation*. Philadelpia: Fortress Press, 1979.

Knight, George A. F. *Servant Theology: Isaiah 40–55*. International Theological Commentary. Grand Rapids, Mich.: Eerdmans, 1984.

Kreider, Alan. *Journey Towards Holiness: A Way of Living for God's Nation*. Scottdale, Pa.: Herald Press, 1987.

Krodel, Gerhard A. *Revelation*. Augsburg Commentary on the New Testament. Minneapolis: Augsburg Press, 1989.

Levenson, Jon D. *Creation and the Persistence of Evil: The Jewish Drama of Divine Omnipotence*. San Francisco: HarperCollins, 1988.

Limburg, James. *Hosea—Micah*. Interpretation Commentary. Atlanta: John Knox Press, 1988.

Lind, Millard C. *Monotheism, Power, Justice: Collected Old Testament Essays*. Elkhart, Ind.: Institute of Mennonite Studies, 1990.

———. *Yahweh is a Warrior: The Theology of Warfare in Ancient Israel*. Scottdale, Pa.: Herald Press, 1980.

Martin, Ralph P. *Reconciliation: A Study of Paul's Theology*. Atlanta: John Knox Press, 1981.

Martin-Achard, Robert. *God's People in Crisis: Amos*. International Theological Commentary. Grand Rapids, Mich.: Eerdmans, 1984.

Mauser, Ulrich. *The Gospel of Peace: A Scriptural Message for Today's World*. Westminster/ John Knox Press, 1992.

Mays, James Luther. *Amos: A Commentary*. Old Testament Library. Philadelphia: Westminster Press, 1969.

McConnell, Frank, ed. *The Bible and the Narrative Tradition*. New York: Oxford University Press, 1986.

Mendenhall, George E. "The Monarchy." *Interpretation*. 29 (1975), 155-170.

———. *The Tenth Generation: The Origins of the Biblical Tradition*. Baltimore: Johns Hopkins University Press, 1973.

Miller, Patrick D. *Deuteronomy*. Interpretation Commentary. Louisville: John Knox Press, 1990.

Minear, Paul S. *Commands of Christ: Authority and Implications*. Nashville: Abingdon Press, 1972.

Miranda, José. *Marx and the Bible: A Critique of the Philosophy of Oppression*. Maryknoll, N.Y.: Orbis Books, 1974.

Moyers, Bill, ed. *Genesis: A Living Conversation.* New York: Doubleday, 1996.

Murphy-O'Connor, Jerome. *Paul: A Critical Life.* New York: Oxford University Press, 1996.

Myers, Ched. *Binding the Strong Man: A Political Reading of Mark's Story of Jesus.* Maryknoll, N.Y.: Orbis Books, 1988.

Patrick, Dale. *Old Testament Law.* Atlanta: John Knox Press, 1985.

Paul, Shalom M. *Amos: A Commentary on the Book of Amos. Hermeneia.* Minneapolis: Fortress Press, 1991.

Perkins, Pheme. "Mark." In *New Interpreters Bible,* vol. 8. Leander Keck, ed. Nashville: Abingdon Press, 1995. pp. 507-734.

Pixley, George. *On Exodus: A Liberation Perspective.* Maryknoll, N.Y.: Orbis Books, 1987.

Polzin, Robert. *Samuel and the Deuteronomist.* New York: Harper and Row, 1989.

Rad, Gerhard von. *The Message of the Prophets.* San Francisco: Harper and Row, 1967.

Reid, David P. *What Are They Saying About the Prophets?* New York: Paulist Press, 1980.

Ringe, Sharon. *Liberation and the Biblical Jubilee.* Philadelphia: Fortress Press, 1985.

Rowland, Christopher C. "Revelation." In *New Interpreters Bible,* vol. 12. Leander Keck, ed. Nashville: Abingdon Press, 1998. pp. 501-743.

Schneidau, Herbert. *Sacred Discontent: The Bible and Western Tradition.* Berkeley, Calif.: University of California Press, 1977.

Schottroff, Luise and Wolfgang Stegemann. *Jesus and the Hope of the Poor.* Maryknoll, N.Y.: Orbis Books, 1986.

Schwager, Raymund. *Must There Be Scapegoats? Violence and Redemption in the Bible.* San Francisco: Harper and Row, 1987.

Schwartz, Regina M. *The Curse of Cain: The Violent Legacy of Monotheism*. Chicago: University of Chicago Press, 1997.

Segal, Alan F. *Paul the Convert: The Apostolate and Apostasy of Saul the Pharisee*. New Haven, Conn.: Yale University Press, 1990.

Spohn, William C. *Go and Do Likewise: Jesus and Ethics*. New York: Continuum, 1999.

Stendahl, Krister. *Paul Among Jews and Gentiles*. Philadelphia: Fortress Press, 1976.

Stuhlmacher, Peter. *Paul's Letter to the Romans: A Commentary*. Louisville: Westminster/John Knox Press, 1994.

Sweet, J. P. M. *Revelation*. Westminster Pelican Commentary. Philadelphia: Westminster Press, 1979.

Topel, L. John. *The Way to Peace: Liberation Through the Bible*. Maryknoll, N.Y.: Orbis Books, 1979.

Trible, Phyllis. *God and the Rhetoric of Sexuality*. Philadelphia: Fortress Press, 1978.

Waetjen, Herman C. *A Reordering of Power: A Socio-Political Reading of Mark's Gospel*. Minneapolis: Fortress Press, 1989.

Wainwright, Arthur W. *Mysterious Apocalypse: Interpreting the Book of Revelation*. Nashville: Abingdon Press, 1993.

Wall, Robert W. *Revelation*. New International Biblical Commentary. Peabody, Mass.: Hendrickson Publishing, 1991.

Walsh, J. P. M. *The Mighty From Their Thrones: Power in the Biblical Tradition*. Philadelphia: Fortress Press, 1987.

Walzer, Michael. *Exodus and Revolution*. New York: Basic Books, 1985.

Weems, Renita J. *Battered Love: Marriage, Sex, and Violence in the Hebrew Prophets*. Minneapolis: Fortress Press, 1995.

Weinfeld, Moshe. *Social Justice in Ancient Israel and in the Ancient Near East*. Minneapolis: Fortress Press, 1995.

Westermann, Claus. *Isaiah 40–66.* Old Testament Library. Philadelphia: Westminster Press, 1969.

Williams, James G. *The Bible, Violence and the Sacred: Liberation from the Myth of Sanctioned Violence.* San Francisco: HarperCollins Publishers, 1991.

Williamson, Lamar. *Mark. Interpretation Commentary.* Atlanta: John Knox Press, 1983.

Wilson, Robert R. *Prophecy and Society in Ancient Israel.* Philadelphia: Fortress Press, 1980.

Wink, Walter. *Engaging the Powers: Discernment and Resistance in a World of Domination.* Minneapolis: Fortress Press, 1992.

Wright, Christopher J. H. *An Eye for An Eye: The Place of Old Testament Ethics Today.* Downers Grove, Ill.: InterVarsity Press, 1983.

Wright, N. T. *The Climax of the Covenant: Christ and the Law in Pauline Theology.* Minneapolis: Fortress Press, 1991.

Yee, Gale A. "Hosea." In *New Interpreters Bible*, vol. 7. Leander Keck, ed. Nashville: Abingdon Press, 1996. pp. 195-298.

Yoder, John Howard. *He Came Preaching Peace.* Scottdale, Pa.: Herald Press, 1985.

———. *The Original Revolution: Essays on Christian Pacifism.* Scottdale, Pa.: Herald Press, 1971.

———. *The Politics of Jesus.* 2nd. ed. Grand Rapids, Mich.: Eerdmans, 1994.

Yoder, Perry B. *Shalom: The Bible's Word for Salvation, Justice, and Peace.* Newton, Kan: Faith and Life Press, 1987.

Zehr, Howard. *Changing Lenses: A New Focus for Crime and Justice.* Scottdale, Pa.: Herald Press, 1990.

# The Author

*T*ED GRIMSRUD TEACHES THEOLOGY and peace studies at Eastern Mennonite University, Harrisonburg, Virginia. Prior to joining the EMU faculty, he served for ten years as a Mennonite pastor in Oregon, Arizona, and South Dakota.

Grimsrud holds an M.A. in Peace Studies from Associated Mennonite Biblical Seminary and a Ph.D. in Christian Ethics from the Graduate Theological Union. He is author of *Triumph of the Lamb: A Self-Study Guide to the Book of Revelation* (Herald Press, 1987).

He lives in Harrisonburg with his wife, Kathleen Temple, and teenage son Johan Grimsrud. He is a member of Shalom Mennonite Church.